Cricut
Expression®

Cricut Expression®

A Comprehensive Guide to Creating with Your Machine

Cathie Rigby

GIBBS SMITH
TO ENRICH AND INSPIRE HUMANKIND

First Edition
16 15 14 13 12   5 4 3 2

Text © 2012 Gibbs Smith
Photographs by Zac Williams © 2012 Gibbs Smith

Published by
Gibbs Smith
P.O. Box 667
Layton, Utah 84041

1.800.835.4993 orders
www.gibbs-smith.com

Designed by Cherie Hanson
Printed and bound in China
Gibbs Smith books are printed on either recycled, 100% post-consumer waste, FSC-certified papers or on paper produced from sustainable PEFC-certified forest/controlled wood source. Learn more at www.pefc.org.

Library of Congress Cataloging-in-Publication Data

Rigby, Cathie.
  Cricut Expression : A Comprehensive Guide to Creating with Your Machine / Cathie Rigby. — First edition.
    pages cm
  ISBN 978-1-4236-2310-6
1. Paperwork—Technique. 2. Cut-out craft—Technique. 3. Cut-out craft—Equipment and supplies. 4. Provo Craft (Group)—Equipment and supplies. I. Title.
  TT870.R545 2012
  736'.98—dc23
                              2011046303

Acknowledgments

In loving memory of my dad, Hector Camargo, whose beautifully worded letters touched my heart through the ages and inspired me to preserve every moment of life I can.

Any creative talent I have I owe to my exceptional mother, who instilled in me early the love of crafting. I will always treasure all she has taught me and the many moments we have spent playing together.

Many thanks to my many wonderful students I have had over the years. Their enthusiasm and encouragement helped me to finally put it in writing. To the team at Gibbs Smith: thank you for believing in this project and making a Cricut Lover's dream come true. Thank you, Suzanne Taylor, Madge Baird, and Maurianne Dunn. A special thanks to Anita Wood for that first phone call.

This endeavor could have never been completed without the support and encouragement of my Scrapping Sisters: Anne Burgess, Deanne Wiggins, and Joyce Coy. You have been my shoulders to lean on and the voices of reason in my head. Thank you for helping me get it done and coming to my rescue anytime of day or night.

Special hugs of appreciation to the many talented designers who contributed their work to this book. I know their passion for this craft is equal to my own. To my Creative Cutter design team—Carrie, Jenny, Mollie, Christel, and Melin—your talent is unsurpassed! I thank you for sharing your time and creativity on my website.

No creative work can be accomplished without first having inspiration. Kisses to my beautiful family for giving my life purpose and happiness. Brian, Derek, Samantha, Christine, Jasmine, and Kylee—you make me want to capture every moment of every day in my heart. The pictures of your lives are finished volumes in my mind.

To the person who is the rock of my life, my husband, Kyle—your patience, love, and support have made all the difference in my dreams. Thank you for helping me believe that together we can accomplish anything.

Contents

Part 1: Learning to Use the Cricut Expression®

Introduction

Learn the basics of using the Cricut Expression. Understand what supplies come with the machine, how to set up your machine to get ready to create die cuts, and what other tools will make your Cricut Expression most effective.

Cutting Basics: A Beginner and Refresher's Course

For crafters who are looking for a complete tour of the Cricut Expression as well as those who are familiar with the machine, this chapter teaches each function with exercises and thorough explanations.

Cartridge Handbook Strategies

Understand strategies for easily coordinating the information on the Cricut cartridge with the information in the cartridge handbook.

Exploring Possibilities

Once you understand the basic functions of the Cricut Expression, this section provides instructions on advanced features, such as the modes and functions.

Color, Texture, and Dimension

Understand how to use the Cricut Expression to add color, texture, and dimension to your craft projects.

Cutting Guide

Learn the perfect settings to cut every type of material using the Cricut Expression.

Cricut Expression® 2

Learn the new features of the Cricut Expression 2 and how it differs from the original Cricut Expression.

Part 2: Project Ideas for the Cricut Expression®

Cards

Page Layouts

For the Home

Gifts & Parties

Introduction

Whether you just purchased your Cricut Expression® or you purchased it when it was first released almost 5 years ago, you are undoubtedly anxious to make the best use of this amazing technology. You have made a wise choice because, unlike so many of the crafting tools we buy in the hopes of creating amazing works of art, that wind up stored in a closet or collecting dust on a shelf, this tool can be used over and over again with new and inventive results each and every time you plug it in.

Whether you're a card maker, a scrapbooker, a teacher, an artist, a quilter, a week-end-only hobbyist, or an enthusiastic grandparent wanting new ways to entertain those grandkids, this machine helps you evolve your creative side. I started scrapbooking and card making when the newest tool available was shaped edge scissors. I quickly discovered that just owning new tools wasn't enough to improve my creative side. I only experienced real creative growth when I understood how to use a tool and how to make the new tool work with the other products I already owned. As a Cricut instructor, that is what I try to teach.

This machine performs specific functions, but it also does so much more. Once you understand the technical portion of just how to use it, you will begin to develop the real knowledge of creating. You can start with simply cutting letters and basic shapes in any size you wish. Then with just a few more easy techniques, you can quickly move to creating cards and shapes with layered texture and dimension. You'll find yourself inspired to decorate your home or make that special one-of-a-kind project to give a loved one. Eventually you will find that the possibilities are endless and this one machine with its cutting-edge technology will quickly become the most essential tool in your creative evolution.

OUT OF THE BOX

You did it! You purchased this machine with all of its potential, but now you have to take that first step and get it out of the box. This will be the hardest part of getting started. Once you make the commitment to get creative, don't be intimidated by the big machine. It may be the biggest crafting tool you will ever buy, but don't let that scare you—anyone can operate the Cricut Expression; anyone can create right out of the box with just the touch of a few buttons.

SETUP

1. After taking your Cricut Expression out of the box, remove all tape, packaging, and plastic.

2. Attach your power cord to the adaptor and insert the cord into the back right side of your machine.

3. Firmly pull up on the hood and open the Cricut Expression door on the front.

4. Check the area directly behind your machine and clear all cords or obstacles. Once you begin to use your machine, the cutting mat will pass from the front to the back as it cuts.

SUPPLIES

There are 3 main components to your Cricut Expression that will work together to produce amazing images: your blade, cutting mat, and cartridge. These supplies come with every Cricut Expression, and they allow you to begin creating right away. Each Cricut Expression comes with two cartridges, and additional cartridges can be purchased later as your creativity grows.

Cutting Blade

The Cricut blade is the item that will require the most frequent replacement. A typical blade is meant to make anywhere from 500 to 1,500 cuts. How often you replace a blade depends on how often you are cutting and the types of materials you are cutting.

Let's start by getting to know your blade assembly:

1. Rotate the top of the unit from the number 1 to the number 6.

Notice when the number 1 is over the small arrow, your blade does not extend past the base of the assembly. As you move to the number 6, your blade descends further out from the bottom. This blade setting number controls how far down the chamber your blade will go.

2. Now turn your assembly upside down and press the spindle.

This will extend the blade completely and will allow you to see when there are paper fibers left behind from previous cuts.

When your blade becomes worn, this is also how you will replace blades. Replacement blades come two to a package with a red plastic coating over the blade. Be sure you are careful when replacing blades because they will need to be inserted uncovered with the blade edge exposed. Whenever your cuts appear to be ragged or not going through the paper properly, the blade should be checked before being replaced. Even the smallest fuzzy paper fibers left behind can interfere with the rotation of the blade, causing your blade to appear dull. The best way to maintain the sharpness of your blade is to expose the blade and blow away any fuzzy material that has collected around it.

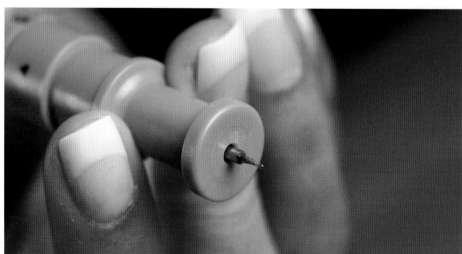

Now that you're familiar with the blade assembly, let's load it into the black cradle of your Cricut Expression:

1. Loosen the silver screw, turning to the left a couple of times.

2. Swing the silver screw to the right, and open the black cradle arms.

3. Insert the blade assembly into the black cradle arms with the small black arrow on the blade assembly facing forward.

4. Secure the black cradle arms around the blade assembly, swing silver screw back to the left, and tighten the screw.

Note: If your blade seems to be floating in the air or wobbly, it has not been inserted properly.

For more information on cutting blade settings, please see the Cutting Guide on page 44.

Cutting Mat

Your cutting mat is included with your machine and comes with a protective plastic cover. This plastic cover has a wrong and a right side. If you feel both sides of this plastic, you will notice one side feels greasier than the other. This greasier side needs to be next to the sticky mat surface when you store it. If you accidentally place the other side down, then the next time you remove the cover, a lot of your tacky material will rip off of the mat and be stuck to the plastic cover.

If you can't feel the difference between the right and wrong sides, listen for the difference: when removing the plastic cover, you should hear a suctioning sound. If you hear a sound more like tearing paper, you have the wrong side down. The easiest way to control which way the plastic cover should be placed on your mat is to write on it right out of the box. Use a permanent marker and place your name on the plastic cover. You will quickly notice if you start to place it on backwards because your name will appear backwards on the plastic. You will obtain optimal cutting results if you are using a tacky mat to properly hold your product in place while cutting.

The Cricut cutting mats are the second most frequently replaced item in your cutting system. How often you replace these mats will depend on how well they are maintained. An average Cricut mat should last between 25 and 40 full cuts. With proper care, you can extend the life of your mat:

- Replace the plastic cover over your mat for storage when you are done cutting.

- Keep lint and dust off the tacky surface to keep the surface sticky.

- Control the amount of paper you use per cut. It is not necessary to always place a full sheet of paper on your mat. If the image you are cutting is 6 inches, no more than 8 inches of paper is needed. Give yourself a few extra inches to prevent cutting off of the paper.

- When placing your paper on the mat, always start in the Home Position of the mat (the upper-right corner).

The default setting on your machine will cut from this Home Position and proceed downward. If you have less than a full sheet on your mat, it is important to keep an eye on your project as it cuts. If your paper shifts due to improper placement or you miscalculated the size of your image, you can easily press the Stop button located on the far right side of your machine to prevent cuts onto the mat. Rotation of your cutting mat will also help wear out the mat more evenly. To accomplish this simply rotate between the 2 sides that are able to load into your machine. One end has a large green arrow and the other has a cutout shape to hang your mat.

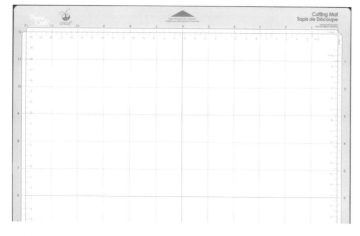

This will allow Home Position, the most frequently used corner, to last longer.

Cartridges

Cartridges are probably the accessory you will enjoy the most! The variety and quality of artwork is unbelievable, and I know you'll want to find your favorites, but before you decide which ones will be on your wish list, take a moment to review this section and make yourself aware of just what each cartridge type provides. Each cartridge comes with a keypad overlay, which will be explained later.

Most Cricut Expression machines include 1 or 2 cartridges with purchase. The most common combination is Accent Essentials and Plantin Schoolbook. If your machine included different cartridges, but you would still like these 2 specific cartridges, you may be able to use the Cricut Rewards Program to bank points and receive them for the cost of shipping. For more information on the Cricut Rewards Program, visit CricutRewards.com.

Boxed Cartridge. All boxed cartridges have 2 things in common: a spiral-bound handbook and 6 creative feature keys unique to each cartridge. I like to think of creative feature keys as the place where the magic happens. With the exception of the shadow and blackout features, almost all creative feature keys add additional images or layers to your collection. By activating a creative feature key, you open the keypad to another 2 images per button or a whole new set of 100 characters. A basic boxed cartridge is the most extensive cartridge and can hold up to 700 different shapes, images, or lettering styles—100 per creative feature key and 100 base characters. Once you appreciate all of this versatility, your creative adventure truly begins!

There are 3 types of boxed cartridges, and each type is color-coded:

1. **Font cartridges** are peach.

Font cartridges contain lettering options. Some cartridges contain only one font style and others will include variations or multiple font styles within 1 font cartridge. For example, Lyrical Letters contains 7 different font styles in 1 cartridge.

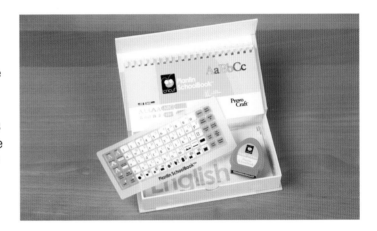

2. **Shapes cartridges** are light blue.

Shapes cartridges contain theme-related characters that coordinate with one another. Holidays, special occasions, and licensed cartoon characters are just a few of the many different themes represented with a shapes cartridge. These may or may not include a font, but when they do, the lettering style is related to the theme of the cartridge.

3. **Classmates cartridges** are green.
Classmate cartridges are educationally based cartridges created to make learning fun. These cartridges can be used by educators, schools, and parents to teach children how to read, learn geography, become familiar with their community, and learn history. These cartridges are perfect for creating bulletin boards, teaching aids, and children's book reports.

Solutions Cartridges. Solutions cartridges are quickly recognized because they are missing one obvious feature that boxed cartridges have—the box. Solutions cartridges come with an image pamphlet instead of a spiral-bound handbook and the keypad overlay. Each solutions cartridge has two creative feature buttons, and they are always shadow and blackout. With solutions cartridges, you are buying a narrow theme or font style with 100 characters. The shadow and blackout keys offer only a layer to the basic keys and no additional shapes. Because these cartridges offer fewer options, they are less expensive.

Note: Many of these cartridges have been discontinued, but the Event Cartridges introduced in 2011 are very similar.

Seasonal Cartridges. Seasonal cartridges are typically released quarterly, and they are the least expensive cartridge type. These cartridges come as a limited release and are available only while supplies last. They do not come in a box and are marked with a bold color stripe to make you aware they are different than other cartridges. There are three things to know when buying this type of cartridge:
1. They include a back card instead of a spiral-bound handbook to show you how to create each image.
2. They come with no creative feature buttons.
3. They include between 10 and 50 finished images.

In cartridges that have only 10 finished projects, there will likely be several layers and shadow options available. These cartridges include special holiday characters, and knowing they are available for a limited time makes them a collector's choice.

Cricut Lite. Cricut Lite was added in 2010 as a Walmart-exclusive brand. These cartridges can only be purchased through Walmart stores, and they have some unique features:

1. They come in a plastic box.
2. They include a trifold card with an instructional breakdown of the layers.
3. The keypad has one creative feature button that adds additional shapes, layers, or words.

Cricut Cake®. A new addition to the Cricut cutting world was released in 2010: the Cricut Cake. These new cartridges are a variation of the box cartridges but are designed specifically for the Cricut Cake. This is a small category but the variety of words, shapes, flourishes, and accents are incredible, and they cut just as easily on your Cricut Expression.

Cricut Circle®. This last cartridge type is similar to the boxed cartridge. The only difference is that Cricut Circle cartridges are available to Cricut Circle members only. There are four of these cartridges released quarterly each year to active members of the Cricut Circle. Membership in Cricut Circle is fee-based. For more information on joining the Cricut Circle, visit Cricut.com.

Plantin SchoolBook™

Keypad Overlay. Notice that the center section has 5 rows of 10 white buttons. These are the image keys. Each of these buttons can have up to 2 characters on them for a total of 100 possible images. You can cut the black character on the button by pressing that button, or you can cut the gray character by pressing the Shift button (in the lower-left corner of the keypad) until the green light appears. Then press the image key you want to cut.

When any feature button is selected, it will glow with a light behind it to let you know which key is active.

KEY INGREDIENTS

Now that you understand the basic supplies needed to use your Cricut Expression, let me tell you about some other items that will make your cutting experience even better. I consider them to be key ingredients because they make a difference in the quality of your project. You will find they make managing the cuts and assembling your layers so much easier. These products are really inexpensive to purchase, and they make a world of difference to your end result.

Spatula. This tool will help you remove paper from the mat without curling it, and it will make removing cut images from the tacky mat so much easier. Also, using the spatula to clean off leftover bits of paper from the mat will prevent damage to subsequent cuts. Avoid using your fingers to remove paper from the mat as this could scrape off or dull the tacky surface.

Glue Pen and Sticker Maker. Once you have started cutting with your Cricut, you will need a way to adhere your cut images to your project. You can, of course, use your favorite adhesives or glue, but for really small images nothing works better than a glue pen. The ballpoint pen style makes putting glue on those tiny shapes and letters so easy. One other adhesive that works really well with small shapes or letters is a sticker maker. This small adhesive machine allows you to apply permanent or repositionable adhesive to items up to 1.5" wide.

Cricut Tool Kit. The next key ingredient to consider purchasing is the Cricut Tool Kit. There are two kit options available: one is the 7-piece Cricut zippered tool kit and the other is an 11-piece magnetic closure premium tool kit. The premium version tool kit includes 2 spatulas, one with the standard wide base and the second with a narrow rounded tip. A tool kit will help you preserve the life of your cutting mat and make removing your cut images much easier.

Archival Black Pen. Many of the Cricut images come with contour lines that add detail to your characters. Using a black pen to highlight and enhance these lines adds a finishing touch to your cut pieces.

LET'S GET CUTTING

Now that you've been introduced to your machine, it's time to get a little personal. Make sure you have completed all the steps for proper setup and be sure to have your supplies ready. If you are a first-time Cricut user, it may be easier for you to learn by going through a series of exercises with buttons and functions explained along the way. However, if you are looking for a refresher course, you may not need all of the examples and explanation. Because of that, the next chapter covers information for beginners as well as those who need to refresh their memory.

Cutting Basics: A Beginner and Refresher's Course

Each of the cutting exercises throughout this book will help you become familiar with the basic Cricut keypad buttons. These basic buttons are the same on every Cricut cartridge. Once you understand how to use these buttons and the shortcuts they provide, creating becomes a snap.

CUTTING EXERCISE: LOAD PAPER, UNLOAD PAPER, SHIFT, AND SHIFT LOCK

Materials
- Regular cardstock
- Plantin Schoolbook Cartridge or other font cartridge

Part 1

1. Place a 4" x 12" piece of cardstock on the mat in **Home Position.**

2. Plug in the Plantin Schoolbook cartridge (or any font cartridge) and place the keypad overlay in place on the top of the machine.

3. Turn on the machine.

4. Set the blade to 5, the speed to 4, and the pressure to 5.

5. Change the **Size Dial** on the far right to 2".

Note: The #2 will appear above the size on the display screen.

6. Hold the mat firmly with both hands and slide the mat under the blade.

Note: Your mat should be aligned with the left side of the machine.

7. With the mat now in position, press the **Load Paper** button and help to guide the mat as it loads.

Note: Do not let go of the mat until after you have pressed the Load Paper button. Letting go before pressing Load Paper could cause the machine to load incorrectly. If this occurs, press Unload Paper and restart the loading process.

8. Type the word "welcome" on the keypad.

9. Press the **Cut** button.

If you would like to use uppercase letters and they are included on the font cartridge you are using, you will see the uppercase option on the top half of each button. In order for your machine to cut these characters, you must first press the Shift button. Let's practice this.

1. Press the **Shift** button and remove your finger.

Note: The Shift button does not work properly if you try to hold it down.

2. Type "W" on the keypad.

Note: You will notice the Shift button light turn off once you type one letter. This means that the Shift button is a single-use button.

3. Press the **Shift Lock** button. Continue typing the letters on the keypad—"ELCOME".

Note: You will see that the Shift Lock button is still on. Press the button again to have the button turn off. The Shift Lock is a multiple-use button and will stay active until you turn it off.

As you can see, Cricut has two different buttons to capitalize a letter or cut the gray characters on the keypad: Shift and Shift Lock. These are the only two basic keys on the left side of your keypad overlay. If you want to capitalize just one letter, press Shift. After you press the letter, the Shift function will automatically turn off. If you want to capitalize multiple letters in a row, press the Shift Lock button. This will keep the Shift function on until you press the Shift Lock button again.

4. Type the word "hello" in lowercase letters.

5. Press the **Cut** button.

6. When cutting is complete, press the **Unload Paper** button and remove the paper and cut letters.

Note: Using the spatula will make removing letters from the mat easier.

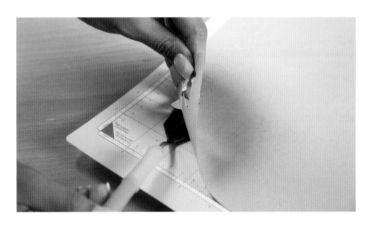

Part 2

The machine has 2 features of short-term memory. The first one we will practice is the last-cut memory.

1. Place the same piece of cardstock on the mat in the exact same spot as before.

2. Reload the mat into the machine, but instead of pressing the Load Paper button, press the **Load Last** button.

Note: The mat should load and the blade should move to a position just below your previous cut. If this did not happen, you probably pressed Load Paper first and have erased the memory. You will need to use the arrows surrounding the Cut button to get the blade to the correct position to resume cutting. Do this by moving your blade straight down, just past your last cut.

Load Last is a great shortcut key when you want to continue cutting on the same piece of paper. You are able to remove images as needed and then continue cutting until your project is complete. If you are switching material or paper in between cuts, this step is unnecessary.

CUTTING EXERCISE: LADYBUG CARD

Materials

- Red, white, green, and black cardstock
- Cuttlebug® machine
- Bloom and Dots Cuttlebug embossing folder
- Sharp small scissors
- Glue pen
- Plantin Schoolbook Cartridge
- Blue ink pad (optional)

Instructions

1. Put a 3" x 12" piece of black cardstock on the mat in **Home Position** and load paper into the machine.

2. Press the **Repeat Last** button.

Note: The display screen will now show the word "hello" from the previous cut.

3. Press the **Cut** button. You will now have 1" letters spelling "hello."

4. Press the letter "J" twice and press **Cut.**

5. Cut one 1¾" circle (page 72 of the Plantin Schoolbook handbook).

6. Cut one 1" circle (page 72 of handbook).

7. Cut six ¼" circles (page 72 of handbook).

8. Unload the mat from the Cricut and remove the black cardstock from the mat.

9. Put a 4" x 4" piece of red cardstock on the mat and load it in the Cricut.

10. Cut one 1¾" circle (page 72 of handbook).

11. Press the **Unload** button.

12. Put a 3" x 6" strip of green cardstock on the mat and load it in the Cricut.

13. Cut a 1" "grass" image (page 69 of handbook).

Note: You must press the **Shift** button to get grass rather than the cityscape.

Assembly

1. Use a white A2 card base or create your own by folding in half a 5½" x 8½" piece of white cardstock.

2. If you own a Cuttlebug® and embossing folders, then emboss the front half of your card. (The card here uses the Bloom and Dots Embossing Folder.) If you do not have a Cuttlebug, continue to step 3.

3. Glue the edge of the 1¾" circle onto the 1" black circle to create a ladybug head and body.

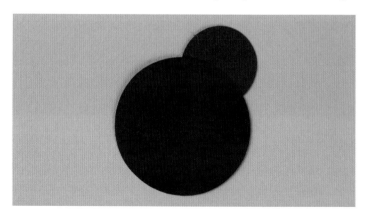

4. Cut the red circle in half.

5. Glue both red halves overlapping at the top of 1¾" black circle to form ladybug wings.

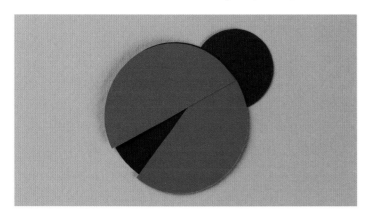

6. Glue the small black circles to the red wings to create dots.

7. Turn the Js upside down and glue them to the 1" black circle (ladybug head) to form the antennae.

8. Add a small rhinestone to each tip of the antennae.

9. Glue the grass image to the bottom of the card, and trim the excess with scissors.

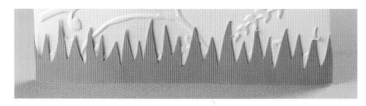

10. Glue the ladybug on the left side of the card.

Tip: Try using dimensional adhesive to raise the ladybug image off the card.

11. Glue the letters for "hello" on the right side of the card.

12. Distress the top edge of the card with a blue inkpad for added detail.

Another basic button is the Sound On/Off button. Pressing this button will turn off the chirping sound you hear as you press all the other keys on the keypad. Once you have turned this off or on, you have changed the default setting. Every time you start the machine, it will have the setting you last used activated.

The Repeat Last button used in this exercise is the second short-term memory feature the machine has. This will be a very useful shortcut key as you learn to create with the Cricut Expression. Anytime you load images to the display screen and then press Cut, you are updating this memory. You will find this a useful way to fix cuts that didn't go all the way through the paper or to cut a different size of an image that was cut the wrong size. If either of these happens, do the following:

- Adjust the settings so they are accurate.

- Press the **Repeat Last** button.

Note: Pressing this button quickly puts all the same characters back on the display screen. If cutting only one image at a time, this feature is not that impressive. But if cutting many images or letters, you will see that pressing just one button is a time saver.

TOOL BASICS

Hopefully, you are beginning to feel some of the crafting possibilities. The Cricut Expression is a useful tool, much like a drill, an oven, a stand mixer, or a computer—the more we understand how to use it, the more we find we can do with it.

THE CRICUT WAY

The next step is to understand the Cricut Way of cutting. When you are using your machines, you are in Cricut World. Once you understand the rules of the world, life is easy.

Rule #1: Understand the cut pattern on your Cricut. In the first cutting exercise, you probably noticed the direction the characters were cut on the mat. All images cut from the top of the mat downward, and they appear to be lying on their sides. This is known as Landscape Mode and it is your machine's default setting. Becoming familiar with the direction of every cut will help you plan the amount of paper needed for your characters.

If you want your machine to cut from left to right, you can change the default mode by selecting the Portrait button.

Tip: Add 2" of paper (or vinyl) to the total size of the images being cut so the cutting blade won't go off the edges of your paper.

Rule #2: Know how much paper to use. A good rule of thumb is to use paper that is 2" larger than the images being cut. For example, if you need to cut a 4" flower, use a 6" x 6" piece of paper on your mat.

Rule #3: Understand that the Size Dial controls the height of your characters. This is an important factor in deciding paper placement to the mat. If you have a 4" x 6" paper, and you need to cut a 5" letter, place your paper in a horizontal direction on your mat to avoid cutting off of the paper.

Rule #4: Be patient with your Cricut Expression. Your machine has an hourglass that appears on your display screen as you make character selections. This hourglass shape indicates that your Cricut Expression is processing the information you entered. Moving too quickly will cause Cricut to ignore the next character you enter. If you ever press the Cut button and the machine does not cut your images, then check your display screen to be sure the hourglass shape has cleared before you press Cut again.

If your Cricut Expression freezes in the middle of entering characters, it is because your Cricut Expression was given too much information too quickly. To solve this, turn off the Cricut Expression, wait a minute, and turn it back on again.

Rule #5: Understand proportionality. It is important to understand that the Cricut Expression cuts everything proportionally. This always happens unless you press the Real Dial Size button. This means the size of the finished cut depends on how each shape relates to other shapes being cut from the same cartridge. The largest image on a cartridge will cut the size you select on the Size Dial button, and all other shapes will cut relative to that shape. This removes any need for us to calculate the size difference between capital and lowercase letters or between different layers of a character.

If you are curious which image is the largest on a particular cartridge, go to the What Is Real Dial Size page of your handbook. The red character is the largest on the cartridge. On the Plantin Schoolbook cartridge page 5, for example, the letter "J" is the largest. If a cartridge does not have an image in red on the What Is Real Dial Size page, all base characters are cut the same height.

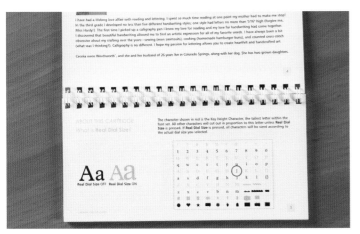

If you select an uppercase letter "J" to cut at 2", then it will measure 2" in height, from top to bottom. If you also select an uppercase "B" to cut at 2", it will measure $1\frac{5}{8}$" from top to bottom. If you want both letters to cut to exactly the same 2" size, press the Real Dial Size button to remove the proportionality. For shape cartridges that have proportionality built in, you will find that the Real Dial Size button gives you an alternate way to use a layered image. When you cut it as part of a layered group, the Size Dial will match the image to the size of the base shape. However, when you want to use that same image as a stand-alone character, using the Real Dial Size button will cut it to match what is selected with the Size dial.

Real Dial Size Look

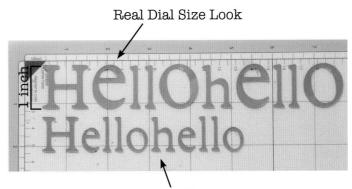

Default Look with Proportion

Doll at Real Dial 5" scale. Pants at Real Dial 5" scale.

Pants at $1\frac{1}{2}$" scale are in proportion to the paper doll.

Now let's try some more cutting exercises to practice elements of the Cricut Way of cutting.

CUTTING EXERCISE: SIZE DIAL

Materials
- Cardstock or paper
- Plantin Schoolbook Cartridge

Instructions
1. Choose a 6" x 6" piece of paper and place it on your cutting mat.

2. Set your **Size Dial** to 4".

3. Using your Plantin Schoolbook cartridge and keypad overlay, select the button with a flower and leaf.

4. Press the **Shadow** button.

5. Press the **Cut** button.

CUTTING EXERCISE: REAL DIAL SIZE

Materials
- Flesh-colored, black, blue, and yellow cardstock
- Patterned paper
- Paper Doll Dress Up Cartridge

Instructions
1. Choose a 6" x 6" piece of flesh-colored cardstock and place it on the cutting mat.

2. Set the **Size Dial** to 4".

3. Using the Paper Doll Dress Up Cartridge and keypad overlay, select the first button, which is a doll body.

4. Press the **Cut** button.

5. Unload the mat from the Cricut and remove the cardstock from the mat.

6. Choose a 6" x 6" piece of patterned paper and place it on the cutting mat.

7. Put a 6" x 6" piece of blue cardstock right next to the patterned paper.

8. Press the **Shift** key.

9. Select button #38 on the keypad (see page 67) to cut a cowboy shirt.

10. Press the **Cut** button.

11. Use the downward directional arrow to move blade to the blue cardstock paper.

12. Press button #38 on the keypad (see page 67) to cut cowboy jeans.

13. Press the **Cut** button.

14. Unload the mat and remove the die-cut pieces.

15. Put a 6" x 6" piece of yellow cardstock on the cutting mat and load the mat.

16. Select the **Headwear** creative feature button.

17. Press button #38 on the keypad to cut the hair.

18. Press the **Cut** button.

19. Put a 6" x 6" piece of black cardstock on the mat and load the mat.

20. Select the **Accessories 1** creative feature button.

21. Press button #38 on the keypad (see page 67) to cut boots.

22. Press the **Cut** button.

23. Assemble the doll from the cut pieces.

Note: The size dial for all these pieces was set to 4". The shirt, jeans, hair, and shoes have been sized proportionate to the 4" doll. You are able to cut a character and all its layers without having to make any calculations or size changes for each piece.

24. Press the **Real Dial Size** button.

25. Make sure the size dial is still set to 4".

26. Put a 6" x 6" piece of blue cardstock on the mat and load the mat.

27. Press button #38 on the keypad (see page 67) to cut cowboy jeans.

28. Press the **Cut** button.

Note: You now have a die-cut piece that equals the size set on the dial: 4". The **Real Dial Size** button allows you to use layered pieces as individual characters for your projects.

BACK SPACE, CLEAR DISPLAY, RESET ALL, AND SPACE

Everyone makes mistakes, and so it's good to know what to do if you press the wrong button. The Back Space, Clear Display, and Reset All buttons help you fix mistakes before you do any cutting on your Cricut. The Back Space button will delete characters you have entered—one character for every time you press the button—just like the Back Space button on your computer. This is most useful when you have accidentally pressed a button and need to change it but not the entire display.

The Clear Display button clears everything on your display screen. This is most useful if you want to create something completely different than what is on the screen. For this exercise, continue using the Plantin Schoolbook cartridge or any font cartridge.

The Reset All button also clears everything on your display screen. The difference between it and the Clear Display button is that the Reset All button also deactivates any buttons you have pressed. The Reset All button function is similar to turning your machine off and on again.

Another button that isn't associated with correcting mistakes but is good to know is the Space button. Even though spaces aren't usually necessary when working with paper, there are 2 instances when you will need the Space button:

1. Creating stencils or using the negative image left behind after letters have been removed

2. Creating vinyl projects (With vinyl, it is most effective to cut entire phrases as you wish them to appear on your wall or project. This simplifies the process of transferring your vinyl to a different surface later.)

Let's explore some more of the basic buttons found on the keypad. Continue using the Plantin Schoolbook cartridge or any Font cartridge.

CUTTING EXERCISE: BACK SPACE

Materials

- Cardstock
- Font cartridge

Instructions

1. Put a 12" x 12" piece of cardstock on the mat in Home Position and load the cardstock into the machine.

2. Set the **Size Dial** to 1 ½".

3. On the keypad, press the letters in your first name, all in lowercase letters.

4. Press the **Space** button on the upper-right side of the keypad.

5. Press the **Shift** button on the keypad.

6. Press the first letter of your last name on the keypad.

Note: Notice that your cursor (the highlighted square) is over the last character entered.

You can move the cursor on the display screen with the 2 arrow buttons directly below the screen.

The left arrow has a minus (-) sign and the right arrow has a plus (+) sign on it.

7. Move your cursor all the way to the left so it is on the first letter of your name.

8. Press the **Back Space** key on the keypad.

Note: This key deletes one character at a time and will erase the character your cursor is on. In Cricut World, you can delete any character you wish, but you cannot insert a character in its place in the middle of a line of characters.

9. Press the **Shift** key and press the first letter of your name on the keypad.

Note: The new character has been added to the end of the characters displayed on the screen.

10. Press the **Cut** button.

11. Unload your mat and remove all letters from the mat.

Let's now practice using the Clear Display button and the Reset All button directly below the Space and Back Space buttons.

Materials

- Font cartridge

Instructions

Note: You will not need to load a mat for this exercise.

1. Press any 3 characters in the white-button section of the keypad.

2. Press the **Shift** button.

3. Press a **Creative Feature** button (Stiched, Shadow, etc.).

4. Press the **Center Point** button.

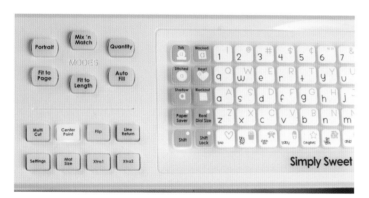

5. Press the **Mix 'n Match** button.

Note: These buttons will be explained in the Exploring Possibilities chapter. For now, we are merely performing a complex cut.

6. Press the **Clear Display** button.

Note: All characters on the display screen disappear. This button is a multiple-character delete.

7. Press 3 more white characters on the keypad.

8. Press the **Reset All** button.

Note: All characters disappear from the display screen, and all active buttons have been turned off.

Now let's try a fun project that will personalize your machine. You will need to have some vinyl and transfer tape for this project. It is also helpful to have a Cricut Tool Kit.

Materials

- 4" x 12" vinyl for die-cutting
- Cricut Tool Kit
- Transfer tape
- Plantin Schoolbook Cartridge or other font cartridge

Instructions

1. Place the vinyl on the mat with the colored side up. Press **Load Paper.**

2. Change the settings to blade 3, speed 3, and pressure 3.

3. Change the **Size Dial** to 2".

4. Type your name on the keypad.

Note: Be sure to capitalize the first letter. Use the Back Space or Clear Display buttons as needed.

5. Press **Cut.** When the Cricut is finished cutting, press **Unload Paper.**

6. With the scissors from the tool kit, cut the image from the larger sheet of vinyl.

Note: This step is called isolating the image. It makes moving or placing the vinyl much easier.

7. Place the cut vinyl on a table.

Tip: It is very important to work with vinyl on a table or counter. Never try working with vinyl held in the air or on your lap.

8. Use the hook tool from the tool kit to separate the vinyl you will not be using by grabbing a corner of the vinyl and pulling it away from the backing.

9. Once you have lifted a corner, put down the hook tool and use your fingers to wiggle the vinyl from left to right to loosen from the cut lines and remove the surrounding vinyl.

Note: This step is known as weeding your image.

10. Use the hook tool once more to clean up the inside pieces of letters, such as the insides of letters D, O, P, etc.

Tip: Make sure the hook tool grabs the vinyl in the middle and not near a cut line, which could damage the vinyl.

11. Cut a piece of transfer tape large enough to cover all the letters of your name.

12. Peel back the release paper until you are left with just the sticky tape.

13. Gently lay this tape over the vinyl letters without making any wrinkles.

Note: Do NOT rub the transfer paper on the letters from this side.

14. Flip over the entire image so you are looking at the back of the cut letters.

15. Use your scraper to burnish the letters.

Note: This technique is similar to putting wallpaper on a wall. Burnishing creates friction that causes the vinyl to come off the backing paper and make it stick to the transfer paper.

16. Peel back the release paper.

Note: If you have burnished enough, the vinyl's sticky surface will be on top.

17. Place the transfer paper with your name on it to the back side of your Cricut Expression.

18. Burnish the transfer tape, and gently wiggle the transfer tape off the letters, using the same left-to-right motion.

Tip: Do NOT quickly pull back the transfer tape from any surface. Vinyl is self-adhesive, and quickly pulling the tape may cause the vinyl to tear, warp, or wrinkle.

Vinyl Tips

* The magic number for working with vinyl is 3. Change speed, pressure, and blade settings to this number.

* For best results, place vinyl on a cutting mat to cut the image.

* Isolate the image from the extra vinyl.

* Weed away the garbage.

* Cut your transfer tape to the same size as the vinyl piece.

* After you cover the image with transfer tape, lay the vinyl on a flat surface and burnish the back side of the vinyl.

* Remove backing paper from the vinyl by working from top to bottom and wiggling the backing paper left to right.

You are now ready to place your image or to place red-striped backing paper on the back for storage. The red-striped backing is a reminder that the burnishing has been done.

Note: You will need to burnish vinyl again before removing transfer tape.

Cartridge Handbook Strategies

Note: All project recipes in this book refer to the keypad button number strategy explained here.

Now that you're cutting with your Cricut Expression, it's a good idea to develop some strategies to make your cartridge handbooks more usable. Provo Craft has recently updated the way it prints its handbook information so there will be two styles to consider:

Classic Handbook Style. This is the original handbook design.

Revised Handbook Style. This is the newer version.

Whichever style handbook you have, the important thing to remember is to use it whenever cutting with your Cricut Expression so you know your options.

Strategy #1:
Edit information.
Within the first few pages of your handbook, you will notice the instructions and explanations have been included in multiple languages. Don't hesitate to tear out any pages with languages you will never use. When tearing pages out, tear out only 2 or 3 at a time to avoid warping the spiral binding.

Note: Make sure you leave any foreign language pages with your preferred language on the back.

Strategy #2:
Number the image keypad overlays and handbooks.
Many image cartridges don't have letters or numbers on the white keys like the font cartridges. This can make it difficult to find the correct image and functions in the handbook. Luckily, the images in the book are in the same order as on your keypad overlay.

Each page in the Classic Handbook has a large colored block on the far left side of every page. These colored blocks and the images on them correspond to the buttons you see in the white section of your keypad. All other images in the handbook can be produced by using creative feature keys. Here's the most universal way to number your handbooks:

- Number each page of the handbook with a colored block from 1 to 50.

- Visually number all white keys on your keypad from 1 to 50.

Example: When looking for button #24, you will press the white key on the third row, fourth from the left.

Note: All exercises in this book use this numbering system to refer to different images and functions. All projects in this book will have a page number and a button number using this numbering system.

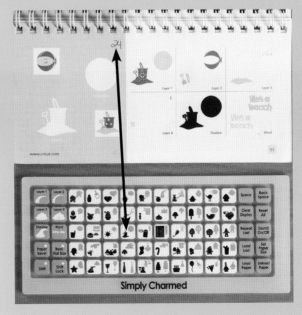

While the design of the Revised Handbook doesn't require numbering it, it's still a good idea to number the book to more easily work through it. One improvement in the revised handbook is the right side of the page. Each of the Creative Feature buttons is laid out just as it appears on the keypad, and all images that require the use of the Shift button are now to the right of the base image.

Revised Handbook

Classic Handbook

Strategy #3:
Develop a paper-saving tactic.

We all want to make the best use of the paper (or other material) we're cutting with the Cricut, and there are 3 ways you can do this: use the Paper Saver button, use the navigation arrows around the Cut button, or use the Set Paper Size button.

Paper Saver (**Material Saver**). When you press the Paper Saver button, the Cricut automatically arranges the characters you select to leave as much paper space as possible. Once this button is pressed, the default setting is changed, and this button will light up every time you turn on the machine. To turn off this setting, press Paper Saver again until the backlight turns off. This setting assumes you are using full sheets of paper every time you cut.

Blade Navigation Arrows. If you know how to properly use the blade navigation arrows surrounding the Cut button, you may prefer it to the Paper Saver function. For many, using the negative space left from a previous cut saves more paper. Once the mat is loaded into the Cricut, you can move the blade to any spot on the mat by pressing the different arrows. This allows you to start a cut anywhere on the paper you want.

Set Paper Size Button. Another great cutting strategy is placing paper in a position that will let the machine know exactly how much space is available for cutting. Try using the Set Paper Size button:

1. Position paper in the lower-left corner of the mat, which is the opposite of Home Position.

2. Load the mat normally and use the navigational arrows to move the blade to the upper-right corner of the paper on the mat.

3. Press the Set Paper Size button.

Note: This tells the Cricut the exact dimensions of the paper. These dimensions will appear on the display screen.

4. Enter the characters to be cut.

5. Press Cut.

Note: If your machine beeps and flashes a message that reads: "Characters will not fit," you have 2 options. First, pressing Cut again will allow you to cut only the portion of characters that will fit on the paper. Second, changing the size of your characters will allow you to get all the characters to fit on that 1 piece of paper.

Exploring Possibilities

Once you understand the basic features of your machine, you can take a look at additional possibilities. The 2 main benefits of using the Cricut Expression are creating larger shapes and creating with more features. These mode and function keys are a gold mine of options that will allow your creativity to soar. Once you have understood how to apply these buttons to your projects, you will move from a beginner-level cutter to an advanced-level cutter.

The manual does a great job explaining what these buttons are and what they do, so I will explain when and why you should use these buttons. I hope you will see the practical advantages of incorporating these mode and function keys into your projects.

MODES, MODES, AND MORE MODES

The mode buttons on the Cricut enhance the capabilities of the machine. Each mode explains the different possibilities available.

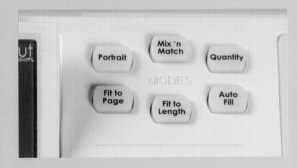

Portrait
The Portrait mode button changes the cutting direction of the blade. It allows you to cut from left to right instead of top to bottom, which is what Landscape mode does. Landscape mode is the default. Portrait is for those who do not like the landscape direction of every cut. The machine will move the blade carriage to the far left of the mat, and all of the characters will cut from left to right on the mat—you will see each image as if reading text in a book. If you want to use this mode, press the button before loading the mat.

Extend the Life of the Cricut Mat. Portrait mode is also useful as a way to control the wear pattern of the Cricut mat. Even when alternating the direction of the mat on each load, you will still have the upper-left corner and the lower-right corner with less wear and tear. Using Portrait mode occasionally will balance the wear on the mat, making it last longer.

Check the Spacing on Vinyl Lettering Projects. If you are working on a vinyl lettering project, you may find using Portrait mode a good way to check on the spacing and readability of the characters as they cut.

These are some things to remember when using Portrait mode:

* You can't use the Fit to Length mode button or the Center Point button on your Cricut Expression.

* The Portrait mode button needs to be activated before loading the mat into the Cricut Expression.

Mix 'n Match

Normally, you can use just one Creative Feature button at a time. However, the Mix 'n Match mode button allows you to change this design option to allow for multiple Creative Feature buttons to be activated at a time. This button also allows you to use the Flip button (which is explained on page 35) on just one character rather than everything on the screen. The order you press buttons is important when working with multiple creative features. If you try selecting the Creative Feature button first, it will apply to the character selected prior to that button. In order to apply the correct Creative Feature button, press the buttons in this order:

1. Press the **Mix 'n Match** mode button to turn it on.

2. Select a character from the white section of the keypad.

Note: If you need to press the Shift button, press it before the white key.

3. Press the **Creative Feature** button you would like to use.

Note: The Flip button can also be used in this step. Remember to turn off the Flip function for the next character unless you need it to remain on.

4. Repeat steps 2 and 3 for each character you need and then cut.

Note: Remember, you can now use different creative features for each letter or shape.

Quantity

The Quantity mode button is useful anytime you want to cut multiples of the same character. To use the Quantity mode, follow these steps:

1. Set the **Size Dial** to the size you want.

2. Select the character(s) you want to cut.

3. Press the **Quantity** mode button.

4. Press the left or right arrow buttons beneath the display screen to set the number of images you want to cut.

Note: When you select a large number, the Cricut will count down the images left. If the number of images selected will not fit on one 12" x 12" piece of paper, then the Cricut will prompt you to reload a new piece of paper.

5. After you load more paper, hit the **Cut** button again and the machine will continue cutting until finished.

Note: The quantity you enter will remain the default number unless you press the OK button after the Cricut Expression has started cutting.

Auto Fill

If you want to fill up your entire mat with characters selected, you can press the Auto Fill mode button. This mode will calculate how many characters will fit on a full page once you have selected the character and size. The Cricut Expression can calculate the number of characters that will fit on a page wherever the blade is positioned on the mat. Another great use of the Auto Fill mode is in combination with the Set Paper Size button to use up scrap pieces of paper. You must complete the Set Paper Size steps before selecting an image to cut, then apply Auto Fill to maximize that scrap piece of paper. For instructions on the Set Paper Size function, see page 30. To fill a full-sized paper with the same character, follow these steps:

1. Type in the character you want repeated.

Note: The Cricut Expression will calculate how many characters will fit on the 12" x 12" or 12" x 24" mats, depending on which you have loaded.

2. If you want to know the number that will fit on the mat, press the **OK** below your display screen.

3. Press **Cut.**

Fit to Length

The size dial on the Cricut Expression normally bases the size measurements on height of a particular character. However, it might be useful sometimes to set the width, or length, of a character or message. Using the Fit to Length mode button allows you to do just that. This mode could be useful when cutting a border image. This mode can also be used when cutting an image to a particular length. The following project is a great example that uses both the Fit to Length mode and Flip mode buttons.

GLASS BAKING DISH ETCHING PROJECT

Materials

- Newer glass baking dish (older glass is coated and sometimes will not etch)
- Cricut vinyl
- Transfer tape
- Cricut tool kit (scissors, hook tool, scraper)
- Glass etching cream
- Brush or craft stick to apply cream
- Timer
- Tap water
- Cricut font cartridge of your choice

Instructions

1. Wash and dry glass dish.

2. Place vinyl right side up on your cutting mat in Home Position, running vertically.

3. Load mat into your Cricut Expression.

4. Set blade, speed, and pressure settings to 3.

5. Turn over the dish and measure the length of it.

Note: This will help to know how much space is available for etching.

6. Subtract 1" from the length to avoid etching over the edges.

7. Press **Fit to Length** button.

Note: This step is necessary only if you are creating a name that is longer than 4 to 6 letters. If it is a short name, skip step 7.

8. Set the **Size Dial** to the size calculated in step 6 (1" less than the dish length).

9. Press the **Flip** button.

10. Enter letters of the family name in reverse order on the keypad.

Note: The letters will appear on the display screen.

11. Press **Cut**.

12. Unload the mat.

13. Remove entire vinyl piece from mat.

14. Use scissors to isolate the cut image from the rest of the vinyl.

15. Use the hook tool to weed out the letters, leaving the outline image on the vinyl. (This will be the stencil.)

Note: Make sure to leave the middles of the letters with the outline.

16. Place a piece of transfer tape over the entire vinyl stencil.

17. Flip vinyl stencil upside down so that stencil is not visible.

18. Burnish the back of the vinyl with a scraper by rubbing in all directions.

19. Lift the paper backing off the vinyl letters.

20. The vinyl stencil should now be on the transfer tape and ready to apply to the glass dish.

21. Place the stencil on the bottom of the glass dish.

22. Burnish the stencil one more time, and remove the transfer tape.

Note: It is important to wiggle the transfer tape off the vinyl in a left-to-right motion to avoid losing small images or ripping the vinyl.

23. Use the transfer tape as an additional border around the vinyl stencil to avoid getting etching cream outside the stencil.

24. Apply etching cream per manufacturer's instructions.

25. Wait 10 minutes, and rinse off the etching cream.

Fit to Page

If you aren't sure what size an image needs to be but you want it to fit in a particular space, the Fit to Page mode button will come in handy. By pressing the Fit to Page button, the Cricut Expression will automatically calculate the largest size that will fit within a given space. When this button is activated, your machine will ignore the number set on the Size Dial and the display screen will flash the calculated size as soon as you press the Cut button. If you want to know what the calculated size will be before you cut, you can press the OK button below your display screen before pressing Cut. To calculate the largest size possible for anything other than the mat size, first press Set Paper Size. For more instructions on the Set Paper Size function, see page 30. You can also create shadows for your characters when using this button by following these guidelines:

Cutting images based on full mat size (12" x 12" or 12" x 24")

1. Press the **Shadow** button on the keypad.

2. Load paper and mat.

3. Select the character(s) you want to cut at maximum size.

4. Press the **Fit to Page** mode button.

5. Press **OK** to see the actual size.

6. Press **Cut.**

7. Reload next paper for the character(s).

8. Change **Size Dial** to the number shown on the display screen when you pressed OK.

9. Press the **Repeat Last** button.

Note: Be sure the Shadow creative feature is off.

10. Press **Cut.**

Cutting images based on a size smaller than full mat size

1. Place paper in the lower-left corner of mat.

2. Load the mat so the corner with no paper is in Home Position.

3. Use navigation arrows surrounding the Cut button to place the blade directly over the upper-right corner of the paper.

Note: Be sure the blade will land on the paper and not on your mat.

4. Press the **Set Paper Size** button.

5. Press the **Fit to Page** mode button.

6. Select the character(s) you wish to cut at maximum size.

7. Press **OK** to see the actual size.

8. Press **Cut.**

9. Unload shapes and place next paper on the mat in Home Position.

10. Load paper in the Cricut Expression.

11. Change **Size Dial** to the number shown on the display screen when you pressed OK in step 7.

12. Press the **Shadow** button on the keypad.

13. Press the **Repeat Last** button on the keypad.

14. Press **Cut.**

Note: It's important to note the actual size your image(s) will be cut if you plan to cut layers as well. All layers will cut to the actual size. This might be different from the size on the Size Dial when using the Fit to Page mode.

LET'S GET FUNCTIONAL

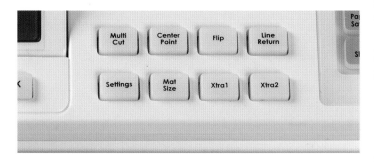

Directly below the mode buttons are 2 rows of function buttons. Function buttons make temporary changes to the Cricut's default settings and can change your blade's positioning and cut pattern.

Line Return

The Line Return function button works the same as the Enter or Return key on your computer. Pressing the Line Return button will add a line break and return your blade to the top of the mat, on the next available line for cutting. If you have not turned off your machine in between cuts, the Cricut Expression will have the height of the previous character cut in its memory, and it will move the blade over sufficiently to avoid cutting into any blank spots on the mat. This button can be used as a shortcut key to move the blade to the top of the mat but not to Home Position.

Flip

Pressing the Flip button mirrors the image of any shape, character, or letter on a cartridge. This button is handy when:

1. Cutting a vinyl stencil or letters for the underside of a glass object

2. Creating a mirrored pair when only one image is available, such as a shoe, hand, or foot

3. Switching objects that are facing the opposite direction you want, such as on a scrapbook layout

Center Point

The Center Point function allows you to cut a shape around images or designs. When you press the Center Point button, the Cricut uses the blade position as the center of the shape it will cut. It is commonly used to cut a shape around a photograph, but it has many other uses. The function is available in Landscape mode only. Here are a few of the ways you can use the Center Point button:

Photographs and paper with an image: Isolate any image right from a picture or patterned paper to use in a layout or collage frame.

Note: Make sure the orientation of the photograph is vertical, as images cut lying on their sides.

1. Place photograph or paper on the mat and load the mat in the Cricut.

2. Move the blade to the center of image you want to isolate.

3. Press the **Center Point** button.

4. Press the shape button you want.

5. Adjust the **Size Dial** to the size you want to cut around the image.

6. Press **Cut.**

Nested shapes and frames: Create shapes that nest into each other without buying nesting dyes or create outlined frames in any shape you wish.
1. Load the mat with paper on it.

2. Move the blade to where you want the center of the nested shapes to be.

3. Press the **Center Point** button.

4. Press the shape button you want.

5. Adjust the **Size Dial** to the smallest size you want to cut.

6. Press **Cut.**

Note: When finished cutting, the blade will return to the same center point.

7. Press the **Repeat Last** button.

8. Change **Size Dial** to a $1/2$" or 1" increment above the last size cut.

9. Press **Cut.**

10. Repeat steps 8–10 for every additional nested piece.

Title Openings: Create a title directly in the center of the 12" x 12" page. The cuts will leave negative shapes on the layout.

SUMMER-THEMED LAYOUT

Materials

- Summer-themed patterned paper
- Coordinating cardstock
- Large paper or silk flowers
- Gems or large glitter brads for center of flowers
- Foam tape or dimensional adhesive
- Cricut cartridges: Plantin Schoolbook, Paper Doll Dress Up, Cricut American Alphabet (found on the Cricut Expression 2 machine), or any other cartridge with a fun frame image

Die Cut Instructions

1. Place the Plantin Schoolbook keypad and cartridge on machine.

2. Place summer patterned paper on the cutting mat.

Note: Remember that in landscape mode the top of the paper must go down the right edge of mat.

3. Load the mat into the Cricut Expression.

4. Set blade, speed, and pressure to appropriate settings for the paper.

Note: For more information on blade, speed, and pressure settings, see page 44.

5. Set the **Size Dial** to 1".

6. Move the blade down to the 6" mark, then left to the 1" mark. Use the mat ruler guide to get proper placement.

7. Press the **Center Point** button.

8. Press the **Shift Lock** button.

9. Type "SUMMER" and press **Cut**.

Note: The blade will return to the same center point.

10. Switch to the Paper Doll Dress Up keypad and cartridge without turning off the machine.

11. Move the blade from the center point to the 2" mark, which is 1" from where it stopped.

Note: You can use the mat ruler 2" mark to check placement.

12. Change **Size Dial** to 5¾".

13. Press the **Fit to Length** button.

14. Press the **Tabs** creative feature key.

15. Press button #50 (last white button on the keypad) to get the grass border image.

16. Press **Cut**.

17. Unload mat and remove paper.

18. Put an 8" x 4" piece of green cardstock on mat and load.

19. Press **Repeat Last** button and **Cut**.

20. Put a 6" x 6" piece of green cardstock on mat and load.

21. Change **Size Dial** to 4½".

22. Press **Headwear** creative feature button.

23. Press **Shift** key.

24. Cut 2 Indian feather headdress shapes—button #32, page 60 in the Paper Doll Dress Up Handbook.

25. Remove the feathers from headdress band to use as leaves for the flowers.

26. Cut 2 frames from any Cricut cartridge with a fancy frame, size 2¾".

Note: The frames used in this layout are from the Cricut American Alphabet (Cricut Expression 2 cartridge), page 69, image #49. It uses the **font2** creative feature button.

Assembly Instructions

1. Place dark coordinating cardstock behind the patterned paper with center point cutouts to highlight the title.

2. Attach green cardstock "grass" over the top of the "grass" cutout using dimensional adhesive.

3. Glue the fancy frames on the layout as desired.

4. Attach large silk or paper flowers to the lower-right corner of the layout.

5. Attach gems to the center of the flowers.

6. Glue as many feather die cuts as needed to act as leaves under the flowers.

Multi Cut

Pressing the Multi Cut button allows you to repeat a cut that has already been made. When dealing with thicker material, it may be necessary to repeat a cut directly over the top of the last cut.

Note: Before you attempt any multi cuts, adjust your multi-cut settings, as explained in the next section.

Settings

Pressing the Settings button will allow you to adjust some of the general settings on the Cricut Expression. There are 5 menus of settings that can be adjusted. Scroll through the options in each menu by pressing the arrow buttons underneath the display screen. Make selections by pressing the OK button below the display screen. To move to the next menu, press OK. The 5 menus include the following:

Language. You can choose to read display text in English, German, Spanish, or French.

Measurement Units. You can choose whether to determine size by inches, centimeters, or millimeters. You can also choose to have inches increase in $1/4$" or $1/10$" increments.

- **Beginner Cricut users:** The $1/4$" or centimeter setting is great because it has easily recognizable size options. You will be able to create commonly used sizes for card making and scrapbooking.

- **Advanced Cricut users:** The $1/10$" or millimeter setting is great because it allows more size options and more design capabilities. The variety of sizes allows for cuts and projects to be more customizable than the $1/4$" or centimeter setting.

Size Comparison Chart when unit of measurement is changed:

- **When using the $1/4$" setting,** a 1" circle is followed on the Size Dial by a $1\frac{1}{4}$" circle. The smallest size you can cut is $1/4$".

- **When using the $1/10$" setting,** a 1" circle is followed on the Size Dial by a 1.1" circle. The smallest size you can cut is .30".

- **When using the centimeter setting,** a 1" circle is actually a 2.5 cm circle. The smallest size you can select on the Size Dial is .5 cm

- **When using the millimeter setting,** a 1" circle is actually a 25 mm circle. The smallest size you can select on the Size Dial is 6 mm.

Multi Cut. This menu allows you to choose the number of multiple cuts the Cricut will make when the Multi Cut function is in use. You can choose 2, 3, or 4 passes over each cut.

Mat Size. This is one of the 2 ways you can change cutting-mat sizes your machine will recognize. Changing the mat size from the settings screen changes the default setting of the Cricut. Unless you consistently use a mat size different than 12" x 12", it is best to leave this default at 12" x 12" and use the Mat Size function button (explained in the next section) for temporary changes.

Character Images. This setting allows you to choose whether you will see an image you have selected on the display screen. Seeing a preview of the actual shape that will cut prior to pressing the Cut button will help avoid mistakes before cutting.

Mat Size

Using the Mat Size button is the second way you can change the mat size setting on the Cricut Expression. Using this button allows you to change mat size temporarily instead of changing the default setting. To use the Mat Size button, do the following:

1. Load a mat properly into the Cricut.

Note: The current mat size shows on the display screen. The battery-shaped object will either display a #12 or a #24.

2. Press the **Mat Size** button to change to either 12" x 12" or 12" x 24".

Xtra1 & Xtra2

These 2 buttons have no purpose but as placeholders for future functions. If these buttons become functional, you will find information about them on the Cricut website: Cricut.com.

Color, Texture, and Dimension

Hopefully you now have a better understanding of the Cricut Expression. Those creative juices are flowing, and you are ready to tackle a crafty project with your new-found skills and enthusiasm. To help you make the world a prettier place with the Cricut, let me tell you about three crafting techniques that will put the wow in your projects.

COLOR

Almost everything you do with the Cricut Expression involves color selection when choosing paper, vinyl, or other material to cut. There are 3 other ways to add color to the Cricut Expression die cuts.

Inking. In recent years, the inkpad industry has provided as many color options as there are paper lines in scrapbooking. Choose some ink and experiment by putting some ink on the edges of your Cricut cuts. You may be truly surprised how much of a difference just a little bit of ink can make in the finished project. You can also try this technique with paint.

Distressing. Another way to add definition to the edges of your die cuts is to distress the edges. You can do this by curling the edges slightly, gently sanding them with fine sandpaper, or running scissors gently along the edges. This gives die cuts a vintage look.

Cricut Color Inks. These are more commonly referred to as "Cricut markers" or "Cricut colors." These markers allow you to use your machine not only to cut but also to add color to your project. Cricut Color Inks work in place of the Cricut blade. They draw detailed lines and can emphasize the lines you've already cut. The cutting exercise below will help you create some flower embellishments using the color techniques.

COLOR TECHNIQUE CUTTING EXERCISE

Materials

- Accent Essentials Cricut Cartridge
- Cricut Color Inks in any color
- Inkpads in any color
- White cardstock
- Glittered brad or button
- Patterned paper
- Card base or cardstock to make card

Part 1: Creating Die Cuts

1. Load the Accent Essentials into the Cricut machine.

2. Load the mat into the machine with a 12" x 12" sheet of white cardstock.

3. Set blade to 6.

4. Set speed to 3.

5. Set pressure to 5.

6. Find the shadowed five-point flower on page 64 of the handbook.

7. Set the **Size Dial** to 2½".

8. Press the **Shadow Creative** feature button.

9. Press the **Quantity** mode button and set the number to 5.

10. Press **Shift** and button #33.

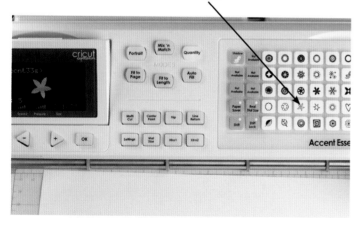

11. Press **Cut.**

12. When the Cricut is finished cutting, press the **Load Paper** button.

Note: The blade will return to Home Position.

Part 2: Outlining Die Cuts

1. Place a scrap piece of paper directly under the blade.

2. Remove blade without jostling the blade housing.

3. Remove the cap from the Cricut Color Ink you want to use.

4. Change the blade settings to what the Cricut Color Ink indicates.

5. Set speed to 3.

6. Set pressure to 2.

Note: The pressure must be adjusted or the tip of the Color Ink pen will be damaged.

7. Insert Cricut Color Ink into blade housing, close cradle arms, and tighten screw.

8. Remove scrap paper from under the ink.

9. Press the **Repeat Last** button.

10. Press **Cut.**

Note: If you have loaded the ink correctly and have not moved the blade housing, the Cricut Color Ink will draw directly over the cut lines of the flowers.

11. Put scrap paper under the Cricut Color Ink again.

12. Remove the Cricut Color Ink and replace cover on the ink.

13. Place cutting blade back in cradle arms.

Part 3: Creating More Die Cuts

14. Adjust settings once again for cutting cardstock (blade 6, speed 3, pressure 5).

15. Press the **Repeat Last** button.

Note: The **Shadow**, **Shift**, and **Quantity** buttons should still be active.

16. Press **Cut**.

17. Press the **Unload Paper** button.

18. Remove all 10 flowers from the mat.

19. Rub inkpad along the edges of the 5 white flowers that weren't outlined with the Cricut.

20. Pierce a hole in the center of each flower.

21. Layer all Cricut-outlined flowers, and add glitter or a jewel brad to the center of the top flower. Fan out the flower petals so they are staggered about $1/8$".

22. Layer all inkpad-outlined flowers and add glitter or a jewel brad to the center of the top flower. Fan out the flower petals so they are staggered about $1/8$".

Note: When completed, you will have 1 Cricut-outlined flower and 1 inkpad-outlined flower.

Tip: The most common mistake is forgetting to adjust the pressure settings after using the Cricut Color Ink, so change the settings before going to part 4.

Part 4: Assembling the Card

1. Use a standard A2 card base or create one with $8\frac{1}{2}$" x $5\frac{1}{2}$" piece of cardstock, folded in half.

2. Cut patterned paper to 4" x 5" and layer on top of card.

3. Cut a piece of white cardstock to 1" x 4" and a pattern with border punch along one long side.

4. Glue white cardstock, with pattern facing down, on the bottom third of the card base.

5. Cut a coordinating piece of cardstock to $2\frac{1}{2}$" x 4".

6. Distress both long sides of the cardstock and glue to card base so the white border shows beneath this layer.

7. Stamp a sentiment on top layer of the card.

8. Attach one of the two colored flowers to the upper-left corner of the card.

9. Repeat steps 1–8 to create second card with the second flower.

TEXTURE

The next technique we need to discuss is probably the simplest—adding texture. Texture is a wonderful way to bring our projects to life. Breaking away from a flat 2D image makes our senses react in a very positive way. There are many crafting techniques available for adding texture to any project, but the one we will focus on here is incorporating a Cuttlebug® and Cuttlebug embossing folders to our cut shapes. The Cuttlebug is another tool produced by Provo Craft that will die cut and emboss with specially created folders. Any of the Cuttlebug line of embossing folders can be used to add texture to your Cricut cuts. The reason these work so well together is that after you have cut your image, you can very easily place it inside the embossing folder, which will hold up to a 4" x 6" piece of paper within the folder, and run it through the machine. What comes out when you open the embossing folder is a wow piece for you to design with.

What is really amazing is that anyone can do this—it is just so simple.

Here are the steps to give it a try if you own a Cuttlebug

TEXTURE TECHNIQUE CUTTING EXERCISE

Materials
- Cuttlebug embosser with spacer block A, and cut plates B and B
- At least 1 embossing folder
- Cardstock or double-sided patterned paper
- Plantin Schoolbook or any other shape cartridge

Instructions
1. Cut one 3" heart shape in cardstock or double-sided patterned paper.

2. Using the same shape as step 1, cut a 3" heart shape in a different color, with the **Shadow** feature on.

3. Glue both shapes together.

4. Open embossing folder and place cut shape on the raised texture surface.

5. Close folder and sandwich between the 2 B plates.

6. Place the A spacer block on the deck of the Cuttlebug.

7. Place the sandwiched embossing folder on top of the space block (should be B, embossing folder B).

8. Slide plates forward so they are just under the bar of the machine.

9. Crank the arm on the Cuttlebug so plates roll forward.

10. After the plates come through to the other end, remove the folder and see the textured shape.

Note: If you do not have a Cuttlebug, you can create texture by wrinkling your die-cut pieces or by dry embossing patterns onto your paper with a stylus.

You will have a Cricut heart with a lot of wow! Try this on other shapes with a variety of embossing folders. You will love giving your flowers, your Cricut animals, tags, and so many other shapes a new life with texture.

DIMENSION

The last technique is dimension. I could tell you to add dimensional adhesive to any of your Cricut shapes and you would be very happy with the results, but I want to take you beyond just adding dimensional adhesive. The dimension that will take you from a beginning Cricut student to an advanced pro can be achieved with Cricut Cuttables. Learning how to use and create with Cuttables will undoubtedly give you an entirely new perspective on crafting. It will also give you numerous adventures with your Cricut, so when you're ready to evolve beyond paper, give them a try.

Cricut Cuttable Tips

Provo Craft has a line of consumable crafting products that coordinate with the Cricut Expression. One category of consumables is the Cuttable materials. These include any material that can be cut by a Cricut Expression. The most popular Cuttable is vinyl, and it is just one of many crafting products that can be cut with your Cricut Expression. Some other well-known products are magnet material, stencil material, and emboss folder material. In addition, the Cricut Expression can cut many other commonly used crafting supplies. Your machine can easily cut fabric, lightweight chipboard, craft metal sheets, craft foam sheets, shrinking plastic material, transparency material, and cling material.

Blade Options

For many of the Cuttable materials, using a deep-cut blade can ensure greater success, but it is not necessary. The deep-cut blade more effectively cuts thick material, such as chipboard and stamp material. The deep-cut blade will also reduce the number of times you need to use the Multi Cut button on a single image. The replacement blades for a deep-cut blade and a regular Cricut blade are not interchangeable.

To improve the cutting quality of thick materials, try these tips:

Use a new or nearly new mat. If you don't have a new mat, use Scotch tape or painter's tape to hold the product in place on the mat. Never put tape on the tacky portion of the mat.

Select images that are solid and thick. Stay away from thin lines, script fonts, and complicated patterns for best results. The Cricut can cut flourishes and intricate shapes on thick materials if the lines are broad and even.

Put the material on the mat in Home Position. Once your material is in place, use the Cricut navigation arrows around the Cut button to position the blade where you want it.

Note: Place the blade where it won't risk catching a corner or pulling the product out of position.

Lower the speed setting. A slower speed will give the blade more time to find the right groove to cut and will help prevent the blade catching and pulling on the material.

Now you have all you need to make this innovative tool called the Cricut Expression your crafting friend. You will be amazed at how many ways and in how many places you can use a Cricut Expression. The possibilities are endless and with some time and practice you will be designing amazing projects that you will treasure for a lifetime.

Cutting Guide

This cutting guide will give you some general settings for successful cutting. When you begin cutting with a brand-new blade, lower numbers work best. Once a blade begins to dull, you will need to use higher numbers to achieve the same quality cuts. The settings recommended here are the average settings for your Cricut Expression. This cutting guide can be printed horizontally, laminated, and placed in the dome of the Cricut Expression for ready reference.

Blade settings refer to the number that should be directly above the black arrow on the Blade Assembly/Housing.

Speed and **Pressure** settings are controlled by the dials on the left side of the Cricut and can be seen on the display screen. When the Cricut is on, you will see graph-style bars above the words "speed" and "pressure" on the display screen. Be sure to check the settings every time you place product on the mat for cutting. This will help to avoid wasted cuts and wasted paper. The number of bars lit up on the screen correlate with the number listed on the cutting guide.

Multi Cut refers to the number of passes the blade will make over the same image. The Cricut Expression can repeat the cut 2, 3, or 4 times in order to work through thicker material. Some Cricut Cuttables require multiple passes for successful cutting. (See the Multi Cut and Setting button descriptions on page 38.)

1 Bar = Minimum
2 Bars = Low
3 Bars = Medium
4 Bars = High
5 Bars = Maximum

Thick Cardstock and Glitter Paper	Regular Cardstock	Vinyl
Blade 6 Speed 3 Pressure 5	Blade 5 Speed 4 Pressure 5	Blade 3 Speed 3 Pressure 3

	Chipboard*, Stencil and Magnet* Material	Stamp Cuttable
		Blade 4.5 Speed 3 Pressure 4

Transparency* and Fabric	Chipboard*, Stencil and Magnet* Material	Pattern Paper
Blade 6 Speed 3 Pressure 4 *(Multi Cut 2)	Blade 6 Speed 3 Pressure 5 *(Multi Cut 3-4)	Blade 4 Speed 4 Pressure 4

Copy Paper	Emboss Cuttable	Cricut Markers
Blade 2-3 Speed 2 Pressure 3	Blade 6 Speed 3 Pressure 5	Speed 3 Pressure 2

Tip: Be sure to check the settings every time you place the mat in the Cricut Expression for cutting. If you make a habit of checking the settings every time, you will reduce the number of wasted cuts and paper.

Cutting Tips

As you use the Cricut Expression more, you will discover some tricks that make cutting easier. Here are some tips for greater cutting success.

Make sure the mat is clean and sticky. The biggest key to successful cutting, next to using proper blade settings, is making sure your mat is in good condition.

- Clean off all little bits of paper before placing new product to cut on the mat.

- Maintain the mat for a longer life by covering when not in use.

- Replace the mat when it no longer holds materials in place when cutting.

Tip: When a new cutting mat is not available, use Scotch tape or painter's tape to hold down the product to the mat. Always tape on 2 sides of the product along the outer edge of the mat. Never use tape on the tacky surface.

Learn to use the deep-cut blade. Knowing when to use a normal blade and when to use a deep-cut blade is important. If you frequently use thick cardstock or glitter paper, try the deep-cut blade. Having this tool will extend the life of the regular blade. Using this blade will eliminate having to use the Multi Cut function.

Follow the speed settings. The speed setting will make a difference in cutting intricate shapes successfully. Do yourself a favor and slow down to avoid frustration.

Understand Real Dial Size. If you understand the section on the Real Dial Size button, you will know how to adjust the settings to get exactly the size you want. If the cartridge you are using has layers, then you may need to use Real Dial Size for any image used separately from the layered group.

Don't be intimidated. Experimenting is how you will learn what works best, so go ahead and try different things. No one will know if it took you 6 attempts to make a beautiful card, layout, or gift. When you get used to the Cricut Expression, you will wonder where it's been all of your crafting life.

Cricut Expression® 2

In April 2011, the Fifth Anniversary Cricut Expression, more commonly referred to as the Cricut Expression 2 Anniversary Edition, was released. This stylish new machine has an updated look and amazing new features to add to your crafting fun.

- Sleek new design with new colors

- Changeable side trim pieces

- Two ports for Cricut and Cricut Imagine® cartridges

- Full-color LCD touch screen with an on-board stylus.

- No keyboard overlay buttons or external dials

- Mat preview screen

- Cutting area light

- Built-in exclusive cartridges (the Cricut Expression 2 Anniversary Edition has 4 pre-loaded, the Cricut Expression 2 will have 2 pre-loaded)

- Longer power cord

- New setting menu

- Mat loading guide slots

- WiFi compatible with a spot for WiFi adapter

- Automatic cut settings and material settings that can be customized

- Separate image sizing lets you cut different sizes with one press of the Cut button

- Multiple mat cutting allows you to plan up to 6 mats of cutting space

- Cricut Craft Room™ and Gypsy® compatible

1. Remove all packaging material from both the outside and inside of the machine.

2. Insert the blade assembly into the blade carriage of the machine.

3. Plug in and power on the machine, and follow the instructions to calibrate the screen.

Note: The stylus for the image screen is located inside the front drop-down panel of the machine.

Tip: If the stylus is ever lost, a Gypsy stylus will also work.

4. The Cricut mat for this machine should be prepared the same way it would be for a Cricut Expression. For more information, see page 12.

Note: The Cricut Expression 2 and the Anniversary Edition machines now have mat guides on both sides of the loading deck to allow easy and accurate mat loading.

5. Load the cartridge on the top back side of the machine rather than on the inside deck.

Note: No keypad overlay is necessary as all button images will be on the full-color LCD screen.

6. Handbooks are made available for the pre-loaded cartridges and are still a great resource to help plan cuts.

Cartridges

With the new Cricut Expression 2, you can load any traditional Cricut cartridge as well as any Cricut Imagine cartridge. Traditional cartridges will use the left-side port, and Cricut Imagine cartridges will use the right-side port.

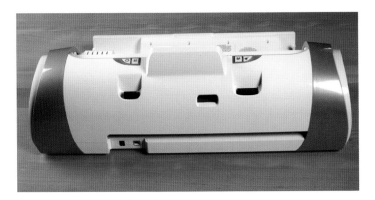

The Anniversary Edition has the images of 4 new cartridges pre-loaded onto the machine. The Cricut Expression 2 will have 2 pre-loaded cartridges for immediate use. To access any of the pre-loaded cartridges, use the display screen.

Beginning Users

In this portion of the book there are 2 approaches we will share simultaneously. For some of you, this is your first Cricut machine and I want to teach you the easiest method of learning your Cricut Expression 2. To accomplish this, I'll instruct you on how to access various functions with the machine while also providing a page reference to the User Manual where detailed descriptions of each icon and button can be found. This approach should help you make the best use of the User Manual and also get you familiar with the Cricut possibilities.

Advanced Users

For others, the Cricut Expression 2 has been purchased after many long years of using the Cricut Expression. For existing Cricut Expression users who are more familiar with the machine buttons in terms of Basic, Mode, Function, and Setting selections, there is a grid on page 60 you can quickly reference the new icons in these categories. Once familiar with the new icons, the transition to the Cricut Expression 2 will be easier. Any changes in the names for buttons are mentioned in the text here.

For all icons introduced with the Cricut Expression 2, there is a new legend provided on page 60 that you can print to have handy with the machine. The buttons and icons are organized under categories according to what they accomplish.

Basic Operations

The first 4 buttons on the machine are as follows from right to left:

Power. This button turns the machine on and off.

Pause. This button will stop the blade in the middle of a cut and will resume the cut when pressed a second time.

Home. This button will automatically take you to the Home Screen on the LCD display screen.

Zoom. This button will allow you a close-up view of images. It must be held down as you tap on a character on the preview mat. Tapping on the LCD display screen again will take you out of the zoom view.

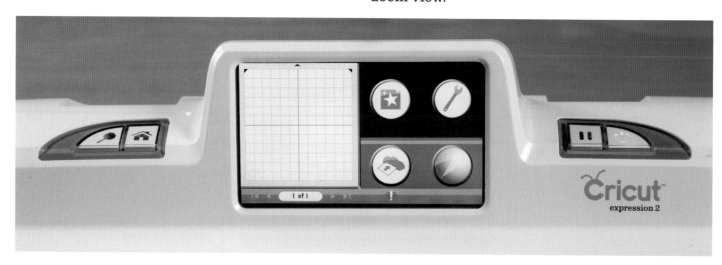

Machine Control
(Pages 11-12 in the User Manual)

Home Screen. You will begin any project from the Home Screen. This is the first screen you will be taken to when the machine is powered on. On the Home Screen you will find the Mat Preview button and the Navigation buttons.

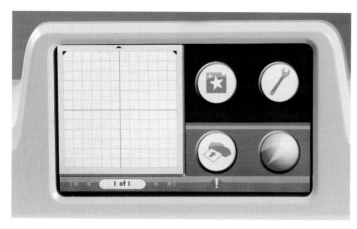

Mat Preview. On the Mat Preview, you can see at a glance the images that are ready to cut on the virtual mat. This preview also allows you to see where an image will cut for proper paper placement. If your project needs more than 1 mat, you can use the mat navigation keys directly below the preview mat to scroll through each of them. You are now able to plan large projects using up to 6 mats. You can also use this multiple mat system to help cut the same images in multiple colors.

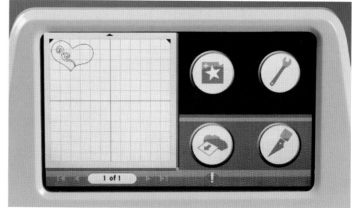

Navigation. Four navigation icons appear on the right side of the screen. These navigation buttons are the entry point for several other modes, functions, and setting screens.

For new and experienced Cricut Expression users alike, there is a reorganized legend of icons that allow you to see the buttons by the function they perform. This grid is found on page 60 and can be copied, laminated, and attached to the drop-down panel of the machine for easy reference.

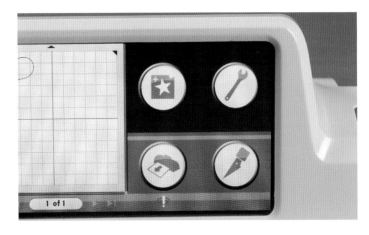

Image Manipulation
(Pages 13-16 in the User Manual)

The best way to become familiar with this new system of cutting is to start working with images. Try exploring these navigation buttons in the following order:

Image button/Image Screen. Once you press the Image button, the Image screen will appear. This screen is similar to Provo Craft's Gypsy® machine.

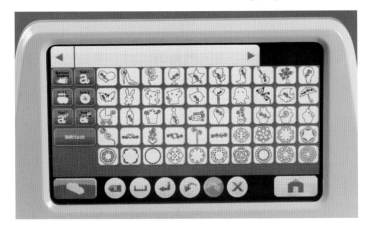

This screen allows you to use a virtual keypad to select and manipulate characters. The images all appear on the right side of the screen and the Creative Feature buttons are on the left side. When a creative feature button is activated, you will note that the button darkens and the images visible on the right change to match the images shown in your cartridge handbook.

Tip: Because the images on the screen are small, it may be necessary to zoom in to get a better look at a character. For more information on zooming, see the Zoom description under "Basic Buttons."

Image Queue. At the very top and very bottom of the image screen, you will see the image queue, or holding bin, for the characters you plan to cut. At the very bottom of the screen, you will find 2 toggle buttons that allow you to switch between screens and some basic editing buttons.

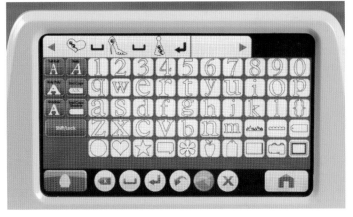

When a cartridge is loaded in the machine, it becomes the default keypad. If no cartridges are inserted, the Cricut Expression 2 will show one of the pre-loaded cartridges by default. To switch or toggle between all of the possible cartridge libraries, press the Cartridge button on the lower-left corner of this screen.

You will then see the options available with an icon representing all cartridge types. The internal cartridges are represented by an image of a Cricut Expression and a pull-down menu in the center. Once a cartridge has been selected, you will be returned to the Image screen to complete the character selection.

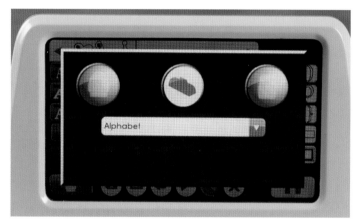

Backspace, Space, and Return. To the immediate right of the Cartridge button are 3 buttons. Existing Cricut users will recognize 2 of the buttons as basic keys: the Backspace and Space buttons. These 2 along with the Return button affect what appears in the image queue at the top. The Space and Return buttons control placement of the image on the cutting mat and can be used to match paper placement.

Undo, Redo, and Clear All. These 3 buttons are the same as on the Gypsy machine and will edit images before deciding where they will cut on the cutting mat.

Let's try some of this image placement and manipulation with an exercise.

EXERCISE #1: IMAGE PLACEMENT AND EDITING

1. Starting on the Home Screen, tap the **Image** button.

2. Tap the **Cartridge** button.

3. Select the Alphabet cartridge.

4. Select the **Font1** creative feature button.

5. Press the **Shift** button and type "C".

6. Tap on the C with your stylus, and an editing box will appear.

7. Tap on the pencil to edit the size of the letter.

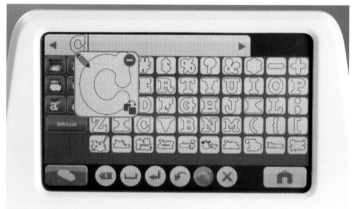

8. Tap on the size button.

Note: This screen also allows you to flip and rotate an image. See page 16 in the User Manual for a description. For Cricut Imagine cartridge users, this screen will allow you to choose between composite and layered images. See page 16 in the User Manual for a description of those types of images.

9. Press the **+** button to change the image to 2".

Note: This screen also allows you to choose 2 image options: **Proportional** (known as relative size) or **True Size** (known previously as Real Dial Size).

10. Tap on **Save** twice to return to Image screen.

11. Now type "ricut".

Note: If you change the size of an image, all subsequent images added to the queue will be the same size.

Tip: Use this feature to select all portions of a layered project at the same time. Entering them together allows you to have the proper size for each piece.

12. Tap the **Return** button.

13. Select the **Font1 Shadow** creative feature button.

14. Type "Cricut".

15. Toggle to the Home Screen either by pressing the button to the left of the touch screen or the **Home** button in the lower-right corner of the screen.

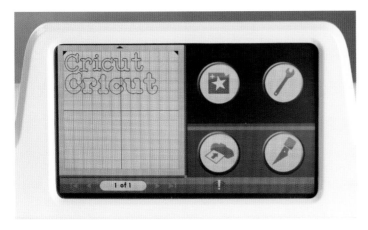

Notice that the machine placed the shadow letters directly under the first set of letters. The first time the **Return** button is selected, you are letting the machine know you want all the subsequent images to go on the next available line for cutting.

Using Multiple Sheets of Paper on One Mat

Next, let's explore how to place images so that we can have multiple colors of paper on the mat at the same time.

1. Tap the **Image** button.

2. Tap the left arrow in the **Image Queue** until you see the **Return** button.

3. Tap to the right of the arrow. If an editing box appears, tap in the center until it disappears.

4. Tap the **Enter** button at the bottom of the screen to enter a second return arrow.

5. Tap the second **Return** button in the **Image Queue** until an editing box appears.

6. Tap on the pencil.

7. Tap on the **Size** button.

8. Change the size to 4" and tap the **Save** button.

9. Tap the **Save** button again.

10. Toggle back to Home Screen.

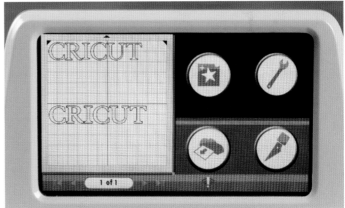

Notice that the machine has moved the shadowed image below the 6" mark, allowing you to place 2 different pieces of paper or cardstock on the mat at the same time. Editing these characters rather than just inserting multiple spaces or returns allows for easier placement of images on the mat.

Tip: In addition to editing the size images, you can edit the spaces and returns inserted in the Image Queue.

Mat Manipulation
(Pages 17-20 in the User Manual)

In addition to placing images on the mat wherever you want, you can also control the mat size, mat orientation, paper size, and start position.

For those transitioning from the Cricut Expression, the first thing you are likely to notice regarding mats is Home Position. The original Cricut Expression cut in landscape with the blade starting in the right corner of the machine, downward. The Cricut Expression 2 cuts in portrait mode. The blade will move to the upper-left corner of the mat and all images will cut facing upright from left to right.

Along with the change in the default starting position, you can now change the mat orientation when working with a 12" x 24" mat. Three key icons will help you place paper on the cutting mat successfully.

Mat Size/Orientation. You can choose to use a standard 12" x 12" mat, which is the default, or a 12" x 24" mat. If you are selecting to work with the 12" x 24", you use the landscape orientation like the Cricut Expression always uses. When working with lengthy projects, such as vinyl lettering, vinyl borders, or banners, this view is ideal and allows for longer items to cut properly. When you use the size and orientation of the mat with other modes, such as Fit to Page or Fit to Length (previously explained in Cricut instructions on pages 34 and 32), you are able to further customize images.

Paper Size. Using just the right amount of paper for any given cut is something many Cricut cutters have struggled with. With the Cricut Expression 2, you are able to see where the image will cut in relation to the mat, and you can also customize the cut space the machine will work within. For original Cricut Expression users, this feature was known as Set Paper Size. On the Cricut Expression 2, when you select the Paper Size button, you will see the default 12" width and 12" height displayed. You can change these settings to the size paper you are working with, and then tap the Save button.

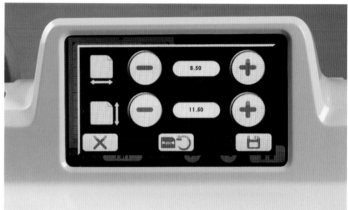

You will immediately see the work area on the Mat Preview screen. The other areas on the mat are shaded to indicate no paper should be placed there.

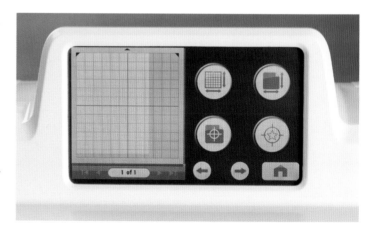

Start Position. This is a new feature that works much the same way the directional arrows surrounding the Cut button on the original Cricut Expression did. With this new function, you can now pinpoint an exact numerical starting point. Pressing the Start Position button takes you to the Start Position screen, where you can tell the machine how many inches over or down to move. The pictured references on the left side of this screen provide orientation to help you match the direction of the paper placed on the mat.

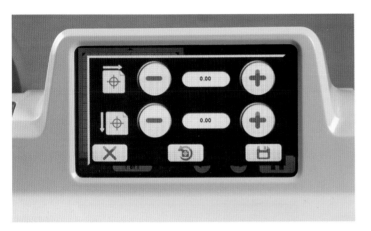

Note: Advanced Cricut users may want to change the default units of measurement to allow even greater flexibility with image placement.

1. Tap the **Image** button.

2. Select a character from any cartridge.

3. Toggle back to the Home Screen.

4. Tap the **Settings** button.

5. Tap the right arrow once.

6. Tap the **Paper Size** button.

7. Decrease the width (top window) to 6".

8. Decrease the height (bottom window) to 6".

Note: In the bottom center of this screen is the **Reset** button for this page. When you are no longer using a 6" x 6" piece of paper, you can quickly revert back to the default 12" x 12" setting by tapping this button.

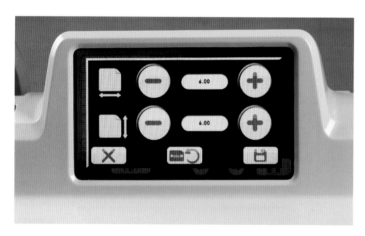

9. Save selections by tapping the **Disk** button.

Note: You will see the image placed in the upper-left corner of the mat. Note that there are 3 shaded sections on the mat where no paper is placed.

10. Tap the left arrow once to go back a page in the settings or press the **Home** button and tap the **Settings** icon to reenter these screens.

11. Tap the **Fit to Page** button.

Note: Notice that the image changed in size and filled the entire available work area.

12. Tap the image until the **Edit** box appears.

13. Tap the pencil.

14. Tap the **Size** button.

15. Decrease size to 1.5".

16. Save.

17. Save again.

18. Tap the **Auto Fill** button, which is directly to the right of the Preview screen or on the first page of the **Settings** screen.

The work area section now fills up with multiple images. The number is determined by how many complete shapes can fit on the 6" x 6" paper. Now that you are able to select and edit images, and choose the correct mat size, orientation, and paper size, the last group of settings you need to adjust before cutting is the customizable material and tool settings.

New Tool and New Material Settings (Pages 22-23 in the User Manual)

The New Tool and New Material features in the Cricut Expression 2 are fantastic ways to make sure there are no cutting mistakes. You can properly set up the machine by using the dial cut settings provided in the Cutting Guide on page 44 to program commonly used materials and tools into the machine. You will find that there are some pre-loaded options available, but customizing the machine will ensure consistent cuts that help the blade and mat last even longer.

EXERCISE #3: ADDING A NEW TOOL

1. Tap the **Settings** icon.

2. Tap the right arrow 3 times.

3. Tap the **Tools** icon.

4. Tap the **New Tool** icon.

5. Type "Marker".

6. Save by touching the **Disk** icon on the right.

7. Save the changes made on this screen again by touching the **Disk** icon on the right.

EXERCISE #4: ADDING NEW MATERIALS

1. From the Home page, tap the **Settings** icon.

2. Tap the right arrow 3 times.

3. Tap the **Materials** icon.

4. Tap the **Settings** icon.

5. Tap the right arrow 3 times.

6. Tap the **Materials** icon.

7. Tap the **New Material** icon on the left side of screen.

8. Type the name of the new material, such as "Patterned Paper".

Note: You can use the up arrow to capitalize a letter.

9. Save by touching **Disk** icon on the right.

Note: Next to the new material, you will find a pull-down list of tools.

10. Select the appropriate tool, such as "Blade Setting of 4."

11. Select the cut speed by tapping the **Cut Speed** icon and using the -/+ to change the number to "4" for patterned paper.

12. Tap **Save**.

13. Select the cut pressure by tapping on the **Cut Pressure** icon and using the -/+ to change the number to "4" for patterned paper.

14. If your material requires more than one pass due to thickness, then change the multi-cut option as well by pressing the **Multi Cut** icon.

Note: For this exercise, the Multi Cut needs to remain 1.

15. Repeat steps 1–13 above for each one of the products you will be using on the machine.

Tip: Taking a minute now to customize all of the settings will mean time saved later when you want to start cutting.

Ready to Cut
(Pages 12, 25–28 in the User Manual)

Now that you are familiar with the Cricut Expression 2, it is time to put it to work.

Cut Button. This will be the last thing you press after all of the selection and set-up.

Mix 'n Match. As you choose images from Cricut cartridges, you will notice that the Mix 'n Match mode found on the original Cricut Expression is now the default setting for the Cricut Expression 2. This means there is a larger variety of images to choose from than before. Once you have pulled images from the pre-loaded cartridges, an inserted cartridge, or an inserted Cricut Imagine cartridge, all you have to do is arrange your different paper and cut. There are so many options to choose from, and you can put them all on 1 mat or organize them over several virtual mats. The Mat Preview screen will help you see how many mats have been created for a particular project, as discussed previously.

Changing Cuts. Many of the buttons that affect cuts are found on the Settings screen. Think of these buttons as telling the blade where to go and what to do when it gets there.

Load/Unload. No project can be created if you do not first load the mat into the machine and unload the finished die cuts. Remember, the blade's home position is in the upper-left corner of the mat. This button is found on the Home Screen.

Load Last. By default, the machine moves the cutting position over after each cut has completed. You can see the next starting position for the blade by returning to the next spot just to the right of the black plus sign. If the image you selected comes out wrong or damaged, then you are able to automatically cut it again on the next open spot of paper. In the original Cricut Expression, this was a basic button known as Repeat Last. Here, it works simultaneously with the Load Last button and can be found on the Settings screen.

Art Quantity. You can enter the number of times you want the images cut, up to 9. Once you select and save the quantity you need, the images automatically appear on the screen to allow you to see how much paper to place on the mat. This button is found on the Settings screen and is 1 of 2 quantity features.

Project Quantity. This is the second quantity option and is a new feature for the Cricut Expression 2. It allows you to repeat an entire project on multiple mats. Once you have completed the cuts on the first mat, the machine stops and waits for you to load the next mat. There is a maximum of 9 times that you can repeat a project. This option works well for repeat cuts that need to be in different colors, different materials, or for creating larger quantities. It also is equivalent to pressing the Repeat Last button. You will find this button on the Settings screen.

Auto Fill. Selecting this feature allows you to duplicate your images quickly over the entire mat. The number of images that appear depends on the size of the characters.

Start Position. This was previously mentioned under Mat Manipulation, but it also applies here for achieving the proper cut. This feature allows you to pinpoint the exact location you want the blade to begin cutting. When this is applied with the next button, Center Point, it allows you to mark the spot you want the machine to consider the center.

Center Point. When this button is selected, the machine will automatically calculate the center point of the image that appears on the screen. It will then cut the shape selected around that point. In order to correctly use this feature, you should also select a start position to correctly place the blade before cutting. Follow the short exercise below to compare the difference between proper and improper use of this button.

EXERCISE #5: CENTER POINT

Improper location for Center Point

1. Tap the **Image** button.

2. Select a shape from any available cartridge.

3. Set the size of the image to 3".

4. Save by tapping the **Disk** icon.

5. Return to the **Home Screen.**

6. Tap the **Settings** button.

7. Tap the right arrow once.

8. Select the **Center Point** button.

The image has now moved off the mat and you are able to see only a shaded square surrounding the mat's Home Position. You do not want to cut this Center Point exercise because the blade will cut outside the paper area.

9. Select the **Center Point** button again to undo.

10. Delete image by tapping the **Delete Image** icon.

Proper location for Center Point

1. Tap the **Home** button.

2. Tap the **Image** button.

3. Select a shape from any available cartridge.

4. Set the size of the image to 3".

Note: Your machine will still have this size saved from the last exercise.

5. Save by tapping the **Disk** icon.

6. Return to the **Home Screen.**

7. Tap the **Settings** button.

8. Tap the right arrow once.

9. Tap the **Start Position** button.

10. Increase the position to 2.5" in the top window.

11. Increase position to 1.75" in the bottom window.

Note: Your center point may be slightly different based on the shape selected.

12. Save by tapping the **Disk** icon.

13. Tap the **Center Point** button.

Note: Your image appears on the Mat Preview screen, and crosshairs appear in the center. If you have a gray shaded area, then a portion of the image has been moved off the work area, and you need to readjust your start position.

14. Place paper onto the cutting mat.

15. Tap the **Home** button.

16. Load the cutting mat in the machine.

17. Tap the **Cut** button.

18. Select the proper material settings.

19. Check the blade for correct settings.

20. Tap the **Cut** button.

Cutting Procedure

Now that you know which buttons will affect your cuts, let's discuss the cutting procedure.

1. Start from the **Home Screen.**

2. Place cutting material on the cutting mat.

3. Load the cutting mat by pressing the **Load/ Unload** button.

4. Tap the **Cut** button.

5. Select the appropriate material to cut. If you have already customized this button, use the green down arrow to scroll through the list to find the material you are going to cut.

6. Verify that the settings are correct.

7. Press the **Cut** button in the lower-right corner of the screen.

Note: The machine will then ask you to check that the blade has the appropriate setting.

8. Check the blade setting to make sure it is correct.

9. Tap the **Cut** button again.

10. Unload the mat or continue to add images for the next cut.

These 10 steps will be repeated for every cut you wish to make. The more you practice, the more intuitive the Cricut Expression 2 machine will become. Since all the features are controlled by the touch screen, maneuverability is very easy.

Tips for Creating

Here are some tips to remember as you start to create and cut with this machine.

All good things begin at home. The Home Screen will be the jumping off point for anything you want to accomplish with the Cricut Expression 2.

Images are the star of the show. The Image icon has a star in the center and will lead you to the location of every image available. To add more options, simply change the cartridges inserted into the machine.

Use the right tool to get the job done. The Settings screen is where you will access all functions of the machine. You can manipulate every aspect of a project by applying these different settings.

Cut with control. When you are ready to cut your projects, the Cut Settings screen will automatically direct you to select the appropriate material and blade settings. If you have customized your settings, this process is easy. The machine will always remind you to check the blade, and the Mat Preview screen will show you just where the cuts will happen.

Load with ease. The Cricut Expression 2 now makes it even easier to start a project correctly. Simply slide the mat under the guides, and gently push the mat into the rollers. Press the Load button, and you are all set to begin cutting with creativity at your disposal.

Machine Operations
(Pages 23–24 in the User Manual)

Many default settings are already established in the Cricut Expression 2 that you never have to worry about, and that makes creating projects easy. All these default settings can be changed and altered to suit particular project needs. You also have access to a Reset Machine Settings button so you can easily return the machine to the default settings it came with.

Calibrate. This will be done when you first start the machine, but you can choose to recalibrate the screen at any time by tapping this button and touching the crosshairs as they appear.

Machine Settings. This button allows you to go to the Machine Settings screen, where you can change the unit of measurement, the cutting light setting, and the language used. A change in the unit of measurement gives advanced users greater size control. Working in $1/10"$ can allow sizes that are closer to many Gypsy files.

You are also able to reset machine settings from here. For the buttons that have default settings, these are the default settings on the machine:

Project Quantity: 1
Image Quantity: 1
Fit to Page: Off
Auto Fill: Off
Mat Size: 12" x 12"
Paper Size: 12" x 12"
Start Location: 0,0
Center Point: Off
Fit to Length: Off
Measure: Inches
Increments: $1/4"$
Light: During Cutting
Material: Medium Paper

Note: You can also find this information on page 23 of your User Manual.

Cutting Light. This is another Cricut Expression 2 new feature and is a nice tool that gives a better view of cuts. You can have the light on anytime the machine is on, only during cutting, or never.

Language Selection. The labels, instructions, and text on the display screen can be changed to another language if you wish. As updates are made available on the Cricut Expression 2, other language options will be added.

About. This button will contain information about the end-user license agreement, your machine's warranty, and, most importantly, what software version of the Cricut Expression 2 you currently have. As updates are made available for the Cricut Expression 2, you can monitor this button to make sure you have the latest version.

Now you are ready to start creating with this fabulous new Cricut tool. It has updated the world of paper crafts to work with today's latest technology and allowed for future growth. You are now able to access all the Cricut family of cartridges with one machine. When combined with the Cricut Craft Room, the machine will give you access to all of the best Cricut Expression technology. The very best part is that the Cricut Expression 2 can be updated. This machine will continue to grow with online upgrades and features leading to even more creative cutting.

CRICUT EXPRESSION® 2 ICON LEGEND

Icons that change the IMAGE	Icons that affect CUT settings	Icons that change machine SETTINGS
Edit	Art Quantity	Calibrate
Size	Project Quantity	Tools
Relative Size	Auto Fill	Materials
True Size	Mat Size	Machine Settings
Copy	Paper Saver	Cut Speed
Flip Mirror Image (horizontal)	Paper Size	Cut Pressure
Flip Upside Down (vertical)	Start Position	
Rotate	Center Point	
Fit to page	Multi Cut	
Fit to Length	Load Last	
Composite-Imagine Carts	Load/Unload	
Layered-Imagine Carts		
Apply All		

ICON LEGEND FOR ADVANCED USERS

Basic Icons	Mode Icons	Function Icons	Setting Icons
Load/Unload	Start Position	Calibrate	Machine Settings
Load Last	Art Quantity	Mat Size	Tools
Paper Size	Project Quantity	Center Point	New Tool
Clear All	Auto Fill	Apply All	Materials
Backspace	Fit to Length	Layered-Imagine Carts	New Material
Redo	Fit to Page	Composite-Imagine Carts	Cut Speed
Undo		Flip Mirror Image (horizontal)	Cut Pressure
Space		Flip Upside Down (vertical)	Multi Cut
Return		Rotate	About
Paper Saver			
True Size			
Relative Size			
Size			
Edit			
Copy			

Hoppy Birthday

Baby Monkey

You're Invited

Great Hunt

Wild West

Sweet On You

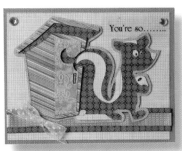

Stinkin' Sweet

Sew Nice

Merci

Piña Colada

Cricut Expression

Hoppy Birthday

By Margie Pagano
Cricut Cuts: Intermediate Level

MATERIALS

- Playtime Cartridge
- Robotz Cartridge
- Patterned paper (blue and green stripe)
- Cardstock (blue, black)
- Brown inkpad
- Fabric (brown dot, green, yellow)

- Dimensional adhesive
- Double-sided tape
- Fusible webbing (1 yd.)
- Twine
- Glue gun
- Glue sticks

INSTRUCTIONS

Part 1: Fabric Preparation

1. Cut a 6" x 6" piece of brown dot fabric.

2. Cut a 6" x 6" piece of green fabric.

3. Cut a 6" x 6" piece of yellow fabric.

4. Cut heavy-duty fusible webbing for each piece of fabric cut.

5. Iron the fusible webbing to the back of each fabric piece, according to webbing instructions.

6. When the fabric is cool, remove the paper backing from fabric piece before placing on Cricut mat.

Part 2: Cricut Die-Cut Pieces

Cartridge	Page #	Keypad #	Basic Key	Creative Feature Key	Shift	Paper Type	Qty.	Size
Playtime	Pamphlet	32	Frog		No	Black cardstock	1	6"
Playtime	Pamphlet	42	Frog			Blue cardstock	1	6¼"
Playtime	Pamphlet	32	Frog		Yes	Brown fabric	1	6"
Playtime	Pamphlet	32	Frog	Layer1	No	Green fabric	1	6"
Playtime	Pamphlet	32	Frog	Layer1	Yes	Yellow fabric	1	6"
Robotz	53	26	Robot26	Font shadow	No	Striped cardstock	1	1"
Robotz	46	19	Robot19	Font shadow	No	Striped cardstock	1	1"
Robotz	47	20	Robot20	Font shadow	No	Striped cardstock	2	1"
Robotz	43	16	Robot16	Font shadow	No	Striped cardstock	1	1"
Robotz	62	35	Robot35	Font shadow	No	Striped cardstock	1	¾"
Robotz	45	18	Robot18	Font shadow	No	Striped cardstock	1	¾"
Robotz	41	14	Robot14	Font shadow	No	Striped cardstock	1	¾"
Robotz	42	15	Robot15	Font shadow	No	Striped cardstock	1	¾"
Robotz	53	26	Robot26	Font shadow	No	Striped cardstock	1	¾"
Robotz	50	23	Robot23	Font shadow	No	Striped cardstock	1	¾"
Robotz	48	21	Robot21	Font shadow	No	Striped cardstock	1	¾"
Robotz	43	16	Robot16	Font shadow	No	Striped cardstock	1	¾"
Robotz	53	26	Robot26	Font	No	Blue cardstock	1	1"
Robotz	46	19	Robot19	Font	No	Blue cardstock	1	1"
Robotz	47	20	Robot20	Font	No	Blue cardstock	2	1"
Robotz	43	16	Robot16	Font	No	Blue cardstock	1	1"
Robotz	62	35	Robot35	Font	No	Blue cardstock	1	¾"
Robotz	45	18	Robot18	Font	No	Blue cardstock	1	¾"
Robotz	41	14	Robot14	Font	No	Blue cardstock	1	¾"
Robotz	42	15	Robot15	Font	No	Blue cardstock	1	¾"
Robotz	53	26	Robot26	Font	No	Blue cardstock	1	¾"
Robotz	50	23	Robot23	Font	No	Blue cardstock	1	¾"
Robotz	48	21	Robot21	Font	No	Blue cardstock	1	¾"
Robotz	43	16	Robot16	Font	No	Blue cardstock	1	¾"

Part 3: Assembly

1. Cut an 8½" x 5½" piece of blue cardstock and fold in half to create a card.

2. Cut a 4¼" x 5½" piece of striped patterned paper.

3. Cut a 1" x 4¼" and a 1" x 5" x ½" piece of striped patterned paper.

4. Ink the edges of all striped pieces with a brown inkpad.

5. Iron the frog fabric pieces together, as shown.

6. Adhere the black cardstock to the back of the frog's face.

7. Adhere the blue cardstock to the back of the assembled fabric frog.

8. Cut five 4¼" pieces of twine and line each up with stripes on the front of the card.

9. Use hot glue to adhere twine to the card.

10. Adhere the assembled frog on the card with dimensional adhesive.

11. Assemble letters with blue letters on top.

12. Ink the edges of all letters.

13. Faux stitch around the letters with a brown gel pen.

14. Adhere the striped paper strips to the bottom and right side on the inside of the card.

15. On the inside of the card, adhere the words "hoppy" and "birthday," as shown.

16. Adhere 3 coordinating buttons in the corner of the inside of the card.

Baby Monkey

By Anita Wood
Cricut Cuts: Beginner Level

MATERIALS

- Plantin Schoolbook Cartridge
- New Arrival Cartridge
- Storybook Cartridge
- Cardstock (light brown, brown, embossed dark brown)
- Patterned paper (blue striped, blue and brown monkey)
- Dimensional adhesive
- Blue ribbon
- 4 mm googly eyes
- Adhesive

INSTRUCTIONS

Part 1: Cricut Die-Cut Pieces

Cartridge	Page #	Keypad #	Basic Key	Shift	Creative Feature Key	Paper Type	Qty.	Size
Plantin Schoolbook	72	41	Circle	No		Blue striped patterned paper	1	3¾"
New Arrival	113	32	Monkey	No		Dark brown cardstock	1	2½"
New Arrival	113	32	Monkey-s	Yes		Light brown cardstock	1	2½"
Storybook	36	18	Flower1	Yes	Shadow	Dark brown cardstock	1	4"

Part 2: Assembly

1. Create a card base by cutting a 5½" x 11" piece of brown cardstock and fold in half.

2. Cut a 5" x 5" piece of blue-with-monkeys patterned paper.

3. Tie a blue ribbon around the lower portion of the patterned paper in step 2 and adhere it to the card base, as shown.

4. Layer the striped circle on top of the brown scalloped circle, and adhere the layered circle to the card.

5. Assemble monkey, as shown.

6. Adhere googly eyes to the monkey.

7. Adhere entire monkey to the center of the card with dimensional adhesive.

You're Invited

By Courtney Lee
Cricut Cuts: Beginner Level

MATERIALS

- Create a Critter Cartridge
- Straight from the Nest Cartridge
- "You're invited" stamp sentiment
- Yellow patterned paper
- Pink patterned paper
- Blue patterned paper
- Cardstock (green, white, black, yellow, brown)

- Clear and black gems
- Character faces stamps
- White ribbon
- White gel pen
- Clear dimensional liquid
- Corner rounder punch
- Pink pencil or chalk
- Dimensional adhesive

INSTRUCTIONS

Part 1: Cricut Die-Cut Pieces

Cartridge	Page #	Keypad #	Basic Key	Creative Feature Key	Shift	Paper Type	Qty.	Size
Create a Critter	68	45	Bee		No	Black cardstock	1	2¾"
Create a Critter	68	45	Bee	Layer1	No	Yellow cardstock	1	2¾"
Create a Critter	68	45	Bee	Layer2	No	Blue patterned paper	1	2¾"
Straight from the Nest	48	21	Flowrpot	Border	No	Green cardstock	1	3¼"
Straight from the Nest	48	21	Flowrpot	Border	Yes	Brown cardstock	1	3¼"
Straight from the Nest	48	21	Flowrpot	Border	Yes	Pink patterned paper	1	3¼"

Part 2: Assembly

1. Cut an 8½" x 5½" piece of white cardstock and fold in half.

2. Cut a 4" x 5¼" piece of black cardstock.

3. Cut yellow patterned paper 3¾" x 5".

4. Using a corner rounder punch, round the corners on the black and yellow papers.

5. Adhere yellow patterned paper to the top of the black cardstock.

6. Wrap white ribbon around the black and yellow paper, as shown, and attach the ends to the back of the 2 layers.

7. Adhere the yellow-and-black piece to the white card base.

8. Assemble the bee die cut, as shown.

9. Stamp a character face onto the yellow cardstock.

10. Add pink cheeks with a pink pencil or chalk.

11. Add doodles with a white gel pen where desired.

12. Use a clear dimensional liquid on the yellow parts of the bee.

13. Attach the bee to the card using dimensional adhesive.

14. Stamp the "You're Invited" sentiment on the lower-right corner of the card, as shown.

15. Assemble the flower and flowerpot layers using dimensional adhesive.

16. Attach gems to the middle of the flowers.

17. Add doodles to the flowers and flowerpots with the white gel pen.

18. Add clear dimensional liquid to the flowerpots.

19. Adhere the flower and flowerpots to the card, as shown.

20. Tie a bow and then adhere it to the flowerpots.

21. Add black gems to make a bee trail, as shown.

Great Hunt

By Anne Burgess
Cricut Cuts: Beginner Level

MATERIALS

- Storybook Cartridge
- Wildlife Cartridge
- Cardstock (brown, olive, dark brown)
- Striped patterned paper

- Brown ribbon
- Dimensional adhesive
- Adhesive
- Brown ink

INSTRUCTIONS

Part 1: Cricut Die-Cut Pieces

Cartridge	Page #	Keypad #	Basic Key	Creative Feature Key	Shift	Paper Type	Qty.	Size
Storybook	66	39	Marquee1	Accent blackout	No	Olive cardstock	1	5¼"
Wildlife	Pamphlet	32	Elk1		No	Medium brown cardstock	1	3¼"
Wildlife	Pamphlet	32	Elk1-s		Yes	Dark brown cardstock	1	3¼"
Wildlife	Pamphlet	2	Reindeer	Words	No	Medium brown cardstock	1	1¼"
Wildlife	Pamphlet	2	Reindeer	Words	Yes	Patterned paper	1	1¼"

Part 2: Assembly

1. Use an A2 size brown card for base.

2. Cut striped paper to 4" x 5¼".

3. Ink the edges of the olive die cut with brown ink, and adhere to the striped paper.

4. Wrap brown ribbon around the right end of the striped paper and a tie knot, as shown.

5. Adhere layered striped and olive paper to card base, as shown.

6. Assemble elk die cut, as shown.

7. Adhere elk to the left side of the card with dimensional adhesive.

8. Layer title on shadowed title die cut.

9. Adhere title to the right side of the card.

Wild West

By Anne Burgess
Cricut Cuts: Beginner Level

MATERIALS

- Old West Cartridge
- Adhesive
- Dimensional adhesive
- Camouflage patterned paper
- Tan cardstock
- Silver cardstock
- Silver brad
- Grey cardstock
- Black pen

INSTRUCTIONS

Part 1: Cricut Die-Cut Pieces

Cartridge	Page #	Keypad #	Basic Key	Creative Feature Key	Shift	Paper Type	Qty.	Size
Old West	43		P	Icon	No	Silver cardstock	1	2½"
Old West	43		P	Icon	Yes	Grey cardstock	1	2½"
Old West	76	Wild	Whoa	Flourish Shadow	Yes	Camouflage patterned paper	1	1"
Old West	76	West	Giddyap	Flourish Shadow	No	Camouflage patterned paper	1	1"

Part 2: Assembly

1. Fold an 8½" x 5½" piece of tan cardstock in half to create card base.

2. Cut camouflage paper to 5¼" x 4".

3. Cut tan cardstock to 4¾" x 3½".

4. Adhere camouflage paper to card base.

5. Adhere tan cardstock piece to card base.

6. Attach a small silver brad to the gray handle die cut piece.

7. Adhere the gray handle die cut to the silver gun die cut with dimensional adhesive.

8. Draw with black pen over the detail lines on the gun die cut to add emphasis.

9. Adhere the assembled gun to the upper-right corner of the card base with dimensional adhesive.

10. Adhere "Wild West" letters to the lower left of the card.

Sweet on You

By Cathie Rigby
Cricut Cuts: Intermediate Level

MATERIALS

- Simply Charmed Cartridge
- Simply Sweet Cartridge
- Black, green, skin-colored, dark pink, light pink, and white cardstock
- Green, pink, orange, and light multicolored patterned paper
- Pink jewel or sequin

- Small flowers
- 2 brads
- Border punch
- Glitter glue
- Dimensional adhesive

INSTRUCTIONS

Part 1: Cricut Die-Cut Pieces

Cartridge	Page #	Keypad #	Basic Key	Shift	Creative Feature Key	Paper Type	Qty.	Size
Simply Charmed	34	7	BunnyCrt	Yes	Shadow	Black cardstock	1	2³/₄"
Simply Charmed	34	7	BunnyCrt	Yes		Pink dotted paper	1	2³/₄"
Simply Charmed	34	7	BunnyCrt	Yes	Layer1	Green cardstock	1	2³/₄"
Simply Charmed	34	7	BunnyCrt	Yes	Layer2	Orange dotted paper	1	2³/₄"
Simply Charmed	34	7	BunnyCrt	Yes	Layer3	Skin colored cardstock	1	2³/₄"
Simply Charmed	34	7	BunnyCrt	Yes	Layer4	Black cardstock	1	2³/₄"
Simply Charmed	34	7	BunnyCrt	Yes	Layer4	Dark Pink cardstock	1	2³/₄"
Simply Sweet	36, 45, 46, 50, 51, 52, 54, 56, 58	22, 12, 13, 13, 15, 19, 36, 16, 19, 17, 1	sweet on you!	No		Pink cardstock	1	¹/₂"
Simply Sweet	36, 45, 46, 50, 51, 52, 54, 56, 58	22, 12, 13, 13, 15, 19, 36, 16, 19, 17, 1	sweet on you!	No	Shadow	White cardstock	1	¹/₂"

Part 2: Assembly

1. Cut pink cardstock to 9" x 5" and fold in half.

2. Cut green patterned paper into 2 strips: 1¹/₂" x 4" and ¹/₂" x 4".

3. Score the larger green strip ¹/₂" from each side on the long sides.

4. Using a border punch, punch a design along one long side.

5. Fold the larger green strip along score lines to create an awning for the top of card.

6. Cut light multicolored patterned paper to 4" x 4³/₄".

7. Attach awning piece to multicolored patterned paper with 2 small brads at each top corner.

8. Using a border punch, punch a design on long side of the smaller green strip.

9. Attach the smaller green strip to the bottom of the multicolored patterned paper.

10. Adhere multicolored patterned paper to pink cardstock base from step 1.

11. Assemble Bunny with carrot image, as shown.

12. Attach Bunny image to card with dimensional adhesive.

13. Add flowers and jewels or sequins to head, as shown.

14. Layer letters onto the shadow letters.

15. Attach letters to the card, as shown.

Stinkin' Sweet

By Cathie Rigby
Cricut Cuts: Intermediate Level

MATERIALS

- Campin' Critters Cartridge
- Aqua cardstock
- Light pink cardstock
- Dark pink cardstock
- Aqua patterned paper
- Grid patterned paper
- White patterned paper

- Brown patterned paper
- Striped patterned paper
- Pink jewels or sequins
- Pink ribbon
- Rub-on sentiment or stamp sentiment
- Dimensional adhesive
- Border punch

INSTRUCTIONS

Part 1: Cricut Die-Cut Pieces

Cartridge	Page #	Keypad #	Basic Key	Shift	Creative Feature Key	Paper Type	Qty.	Size
Campin' Critters	21	1	Skunk 1	No		Brown pattern paper	1	3¼"
Campin' Critters	21	1	Skunk 1-s	Yes		Striped patterned paper	1	3¼"
Campin' Critters	21	1	Skunk 1	No	Layer 1	Dark pink patterned paper	1	3¼"
Campin' Critters	21	1	Skunk 1-s	Yes	Layer 1	White patterned paper	1	3¼"
Campin' Critters	21	1	Skunk 1	No	Layer 2	Dark pink patterned paper	1	3¼"
Campin' Critters	21	1	Skunk 1-s	Yes	Layer 2	Aqua patterned paper	1	3¼"

Part 2: Assembly

1. Cut aqua cardstock to 8½" x 5½" and fold in half.

2. Cut light pink patterned paper 4" x 5¼".

3. Cut brown patterned paper ¾" x 5¼".

4. Glue light pink patterned paper to top of card.

5. Adhere dark pink patterned paper piece to striped piece to assemble outhouse door.

6. Attach outhouse door and striped rooftop to brown patterned paper outhouse piece using dimensional adhesive.

7. Adhere white patterned paper pieces to brown patterned paper skunk piece to complete skunk image.

8. Adhere entire skunk and outhouse piece to aqua patterned paper piece.

9. Adhere ribbon to top of brown patterned paper piece from step 3 and adhere to the card near the bottom.

10. Attach skunk image to card with dimensional adhesive.

11. Tie small bow with pink sheer ribbon.

12. Add bow to the bottom of card, as shown.

13. Add pink jewels or sequins to top corners of card.

14. Cut grid pattern paper to 3½" x 5¼".

15. Adhere grid patterned paper to the inside of card.

16. Cut 2 pieces of striped patterned paper to 1½" x 5¼".

17. Use border punch on one side of striped patterned paper strips.

18. Adhere strips of pattern paper to the inside top and bottom of card.

19. Placed rub-on or stamp sentiments, as shown.

Alternate Color Scheme

Merci

By Anita Wood
Cricut Cuts: Intermediate Level

MATERIALS

- Wall Décor and More Cartridge
- Heritage Cartridge
- Adhesive
- Dimensional adhesive
- Cocoa brown inkpad
- Brown ribbon

- Sentiment
- Large diamond green patterned paper
- Small diamond green patterned paper
- Light green patterned paper or cardstock
- Dark green patterned paper or cardstock
- 5" x 7" blank card

INSTRUCTIONS

Part 1: Cricut Die-Cut Pieces

Cartridge	Page #	Keypad #	Basic Key	Creative Feature Key	Shift	Paper Type	Qty.	Size
Wall Décor and More	37	10	Pear		No	Dark green cardstock	1	5"
Wall Décor and More	37	10	Pear		Yes	Light green cardstock	1	5"
Wall Décor and More	37	10	Pear		No	Small diamond patterned paper	1	5¼"
Heritage	64	41	Cameo1	Frame	Yes	Dark green cardstock	1	1"

Part 2: Assembly

1. Use a 5" x 7" blank card.

2. Cut the large diamond patterned paper to 5" x 7".

3. Ink edges of the large diamond patterned paper and attach to card.

4. Cut one 1½" x 5" strip of the small diamond patterned paper.

5. Cut one 2¼" x 5" strip of the small diamond patterned paper.

6. Tear all horizontal edges of both strips of patterned paper.

7. Apply ink to the torn edges.

8. Ink edges around sentiment.

9. Attach the sentiment to the frame die cut.

10. Pull ribbon through the holes of the frame.

11. Attach the sentiment to the smaller torn strip with dimensional adhesive.

12. Attach the sentiment ribbon ends to the back of the smaller torn strip.

13. Adhere the sentiment strip to bottom of the card.

14. Adhere larger patterned paper strip to the top of card.

15. Ink pear die cuts as desired.

16. Adhere the dark green paper layer on top of the light green paper piece.

17. Adhere the green pear piece to the top of the 5¼" patterned pear piece.

18. Adhere layered pear to the card.

19. Adhere leaf of top pear to the card with dimensional adhesive.

Sew Nice

By Cathie Rigby
Cricut Cuts:
Advanced Level

MATERIALS

- Accent Essentials Cartridge
- Nifty Fifties Cartridge
- Preserves Cartridge
- Aqua glitter paper
- Brown cardstock
- Orange cardstock
- Patterned paper (orange, aqua, orange and aqua diamond, orange and aqua flower)
- Orange mini brads
- Rub-on sentiment or stamp sentiment
- Dimensional adhesive
- Adhesive
- Orange floss
- Inkpad (orange and blue)

INSTRUCTIONS

Part 1: Cricut Die-Cut Pieces

Note: Change Settings Unit to inches—1/10ths for these die cuts. For more information, see page 38.

Cartridge	Page #	Keypad #	Basic Key	Creative Feature Key	Shift	Mode	Paper Type	Qty.	Size
Accent Essentials	79	48	Accent48s		Yes		Brown cardstock	1	3.3"
Accent Essentials	79	48	Accent48*		No		Orange and aqua flower patterned paper	1	3.3"
Nifty Fifties	22	2	Sewing		No	Fit to Length	Aqua glitter paper	1	3.4"
Nifty Fifties	22	2	Sewing-s		Yes	Fit to Length	Aqua patterned paper	1	3.4"
Nifty Fifties	22	2	Sewing	Shadow	No		Brown cardstock	1	2.3"
Nifty Fifties	22	2	Sewing	Layer1	No		Orange patterned paper	1	2.3"
Nifty Fifties	22	2	Sewing	Layer1	No		Aqua glitter paper	1	2"
Nifty Fifties	22	2	Sewing	Layer1	No		Aqua glitter paper	1	1"
Preserves	69	46	Kumquat1	Label	No		Brown cardstock	1	3"
Preserves	69	46	Kumquat1	Label	No		Orange patterned paper	1	2.7"

*Note: Press stop after the inside piece cuts.

Part 2: Assembly

1. Cut an 8½" x 5½" piece of orange cardstock and fold in half.

2. Cut a 4" x 5¼" piece of brown cardstock.

3. Cut a 3¾" x 5" piece of orange diamond patterned paper.

4. Adhere brown cardstock to the top of card.

5. Adhere orange diamond patterned paper to the top of the card.

6. Attach small orange brads to the brown accent frame, as shown.

7. Adhere brown frame to the center of card, as shown.

8. Ink all die cut pieces with coordinating colors, as desired.

9. Adhere patterned paper frame to the brown frame using dimensional adhesive, as shown.

10. Assemble all pieces of sewing machine except Layer 1.

11. Apply rub-on or stamp sentiment to center of sewing machine, as shown.

12. Cut a 10" piece of orange floss.

13. Attach one end of the floss behind spool die cut from Layer 1 with a strong adhesive.

14. Wrap floss around spool, leaving enough loose to wrap around thread guide.

15. Adhere loose end of thread behind fabric die cut with strong adhesive, as shown.

16. Adhere spool and fabric layer pieces with dimensional tape to sewing machine.

17. Cut a 1¾" x 5" strip of orange-and-blue flower patterned paper.

18. Adhere strip to the inside bottom of card, as shown.

19. Adhere orange patterned paper label to brown cardstock label.

20. Apply rub-on sentiment to center of label.

21. Adhere label to inside of the card, as shown.

22. Adhere the larger spool die cut to bottom right corner of the label, as shown.

23. Adhere the smaller spool die cut on top or larger one with dimensional adhesive, as shown.

Piña Colada

By Michele Kovack
Cricut Cuts: Advanced Level

MATERIALS

- Sentimental Cartridge
- Mother's Day Bouquet Cartridge
- Pack Your Bags Cartridge
- Patterned paper (turquoise, fruit and flower, green and blue, green dot, pink)
- Cardstock (white)
- Vellum (yellow)
- Glitter

- Stamped sentiment
- Rhinestones
- Glossy dimensional adhesive
- Button
- Ink
- Transparency sheet
- White acrylic paint

INSTRUCTIONS

Part 1: Cricut Die-Cut Pieces

Cartridge	Page #	Keypad #	Basic Key	Creative Feature Key	Shift	Function	Paper Type	Qty.	Size
Pack Your Bags	70	50	Drink3	Shadow	No	Flip	White cardstock	2 one flipped	7"
Pack Your Bags	70	50	Drink3		No	Flip	Turquoise flower paper	1	7"
Pack Your Bags	70	50	Drink3	Layer 1	No	Flip	Transparency sheet	1	7"
Pack Your Bags	70	50	Drink3	Layer 1	No	Flip	Yellow vellum	1	7"
Pack Your Bags	70	50	Drink3-s	Layer 1	Yes	Flip	Blue-and-green patterned paper	1	7"
Pack Your Bags	70	50	Drink3	Layer 2	No	Flip	Fruit-and-flower patterned paper	1	7"
Pack Your Bags	70	50	Drink3-s	Layer 2	Yes	Flip	Fruit-and-flower patterned paper	1	7"
Mother's Day Bouquet	Pamphlet	4	Flower4		No		Pink patterned paper	1	1¾"
Mother's Day Bouquet	Pamphlet	4	Flower4		No		Pink patterned paper	1	1¼"
Mother's Day Bouquet	Pamphlet	41	Leaf1		No		Green dot patterned paper	1	1"
Mother's Day Bouquet	Pamphlet	41	Leaf2		No		Green dot patterned paper	2	1"
Sentimentals	28	5	Frame1	Tag	No		White cardstock	1	1"

Part 2: Assembly

1. Cut a 2" x 1" piece of white cardstock and score lengthwise at the ½" point to create a flap.

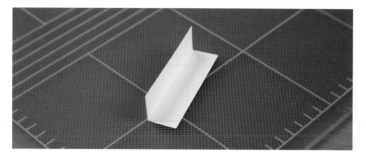

2. Cut umbrella piece off of one white drink glass die cut for the back of the card.

Note: The flipped shape should be the front of card so the umbrella is on the right side of glass.

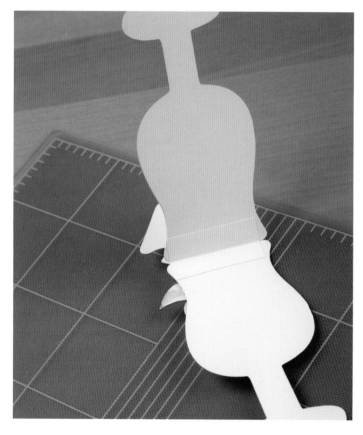

3. Glue flap to the inside of both white drink glass pieces to create card.

4. Adhere blue flower pattered paper to card base.

5. Paint edges of transparency with white paint.

6. Apply small amount of glossy dimensional adhesive to the edges of transparency and sprinkle with glitter.

7. Cut lemon shapes from fruit-and-flower patterned paper.

8. Apply thin coat of glossy dimensional adhesive and sprinkle with glitter.

9. Adhere lemons to top of transparency.

10. Trim yellow vellum to fit behind transparency, as shown, and adhere to card.

11. Ink assembled umbrella pieces with brown ink.

12. Apply glossy dimensional adhesive and glitter to center section of umbrella, as shown.

13. Ink edges of flower die cuts and apply glossy dimensional adhesive.

14. Sprinkle pink flower with glitter and bend back petals while wet to add dimension.

15. Assemble flower layers, as shown.

16. Ink leaves and bend slightly to shape.

17. Adhere button and rhinestone to the center of the flower.

18. Attach flower and leaves to the top of the card, as shown.

19. Stamp sentiment on the white tag.

20. Adhere the tag behind flower, as shown.

Rockin' My Kicks

Look Who's 40

Birds of a Feather

Growing

Short Circuit

We're Family

Winter Wonderland

ROCKIN

1. YOU ARE:

Ⓐ crazy

Ⓑ silly

Ⓒ funny

Ⓓ goofy

Ⓔ amazing

Ⓕ cool

Ⓖ awesome

★ all of the above.

THIS IS A TEST.
THIS IS ONLY A TEST.

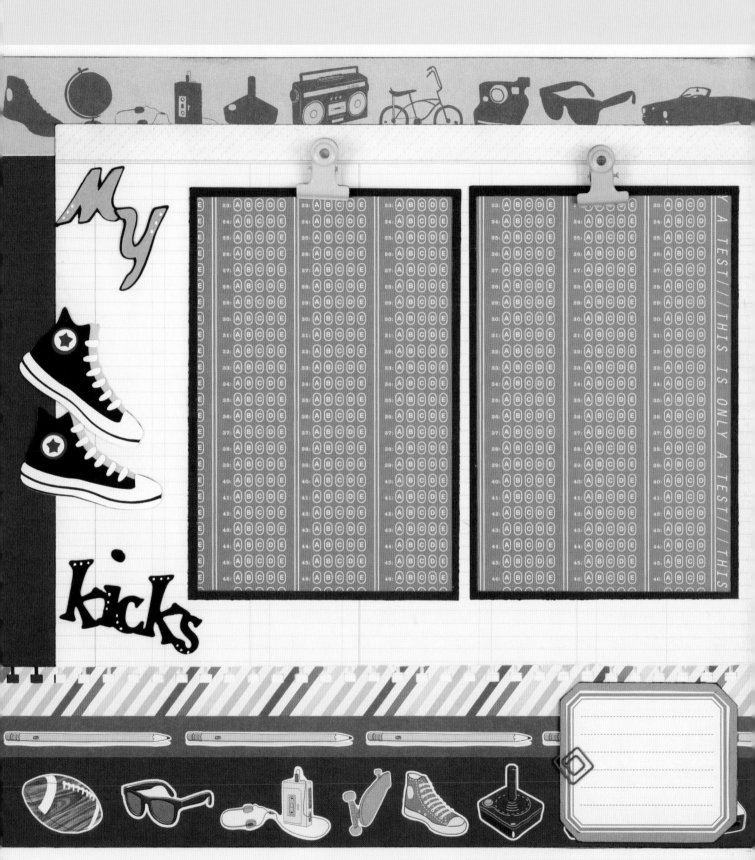

Rockin' My Kicks

By Cathie Rigby
Cricut Cuts: Intermediate Level

MATERIALS

- Nifty Fifties Cartridge
- Adhesive
- Dimensional adhesive
- Cardstock (dark brown, vanilla, blue, black, red, mint, orange)
- Sports theme patterned paper
- Notebook patterned paper
- Striped patterned paper
- Gold star embellishment
- Journaling block
- Metal clips
- Red brads
- Border punch
- Vinyl (black, red, white)

INSTRUCTIONS

Part 1: Cricut Die-Cut Pieces

Cartridge	Page #	Keypad #	Basic Key	Shift	Creative Feature Key	Mode	Function	Paper Type	Qty.	Size
Nifty Fifties	60	40	Boy	No				Black cardstock	1	4"
Nifty Fifties	60	40	Boy-s	Yes				Blue cardstock	1	4"
Nifty Fifties	60	40	Boy	No	Layer1			Vanilla cardstock	1	4"
Nifty Fifties	60	40	Boy-s	Yes	Layer1			Mint cardstock	1	4"
Nifty Fifties	58	38	DriveIn	No	Font			Black cardstock	1	³⁄₄"
Nifty Fifties	58	38	DriveIn	No	Font			Red cardstock	1	³⁄₄"
Nifty Fifties	58	38	DriveIn	No	Font Shadow			White cardstock	1	³⁄₄"
Nifty Fifties	63	43	Soda	No	Font	Mix 'n Match	Flip (on just one cut)	Blue cardstock	2	2¹⁄₂"
Nifty Fifties	59	39	HiTop	No	Phrase			Black cardstock	1	2¹⁄₂"
Nifty Fifties	59	39	HiTop-s	Yes				Gray vinyl	2	2¹⁄₂"
Nifty Fifties	59	39	HiTop	No	Layer1			Black vinyl	2	2¹⁄₂"
Nifty Fifties	59	39	HiTop-s	Yes	Layer1			White vinyl	2	2¹⁄₂"
Nifty Fifties	59	39	HiTop*	No	Phrase			Red vinyl	2	2¹⁄₂"
Nifty Fifties	34, 39, 53, 48, 38, 56	14, 19, 33, 28, 18, 36	R, O, C, K, I, N	Yes	Font			Orange cardstock	1	1"
Nifty Fifties	34, 39, 53, 48, 38, 56	14, 19, 33, 28, 18, 36	R, O, C, K, I, N**	Yes	Font Shadow			Vanilla cardstock	1	1"
Nifty Fifties	57, 36	37, 16	M, Y**	Yes	Font			Orange cardstock	1	1"
Nifty Fifties	57, 36	37, 16	"MY"	Yes	Font Shadow			Vanilla cardstock	1	1"

*Note: You will use only the red star portion of cut.

**Note: After you make the Creative Feature adjustment and change the paper, use the Repeat Last button for these cuts.

Part 2: Assembly

1. Assemble boy die-cut pieces using small Converse® shoes, as shown.

2. Cut 2 pieces of sport patterned paper: one 1½" x 12" and the second 3¼" x 12".

3. Use border punch on top edge of thicker strip from step 2.

4. Cut a piece of 11" x 11" notebook patterned paper.

5. Adhere smaller sports strip to the top of dark brown 12" x 12" cardstock for the right page of the layout.

6. Adhere notebook patterned paper to middle of the right page of the layout, as shown.

7. Adhere the larger sports strip to bottom of right page of the layout.

8. Cut a 2½" x 3" piece of blue cardstock to create journaling block.

9. Attach a shaped paper clip and adhere to lower right of layout.

10. Cut two 4¼" x 6¼" photo mats from black cardstock.

11. Cut two 4" x 6" red patterned paper pieces and adhere to black photo mats.

12. Attach 2 metal paper clips to top of each photo mat, and adhere both to the right page of the layout, as shown.

13. Cut a 2½" x 12" strip of red patterned paper.

14. Adhere red strip to left side of a 12" x 12" dark brown cardstock paper for the left page of layout.

15. Attach a pre-made characteristics list over the red strip of paper on the left side.

Note: This list can easily be created on your computer and printed on notebook patterned paper.

16. Attach a gold star using strong adhesive to the chosen characteristic, as shown.

17. Cut a 1" x 12" piece of striped patterned paper.

18. Adhere piece from step 17 in a diagonal manner next to red strip of paper, as shown.

19. Cut two 4¼" x 6¼" pieces of vanilla cardstock.

20. Attach arrow die cuts with 3 red brads to each photo mat from step 19, as shown.

21. Adhere photo mats to the left page of the layout, as shown.

22. Adhere title and large Converse shoe to layout, as shown.

Converse is a registered trademark of Converse Inc., Andover, MA 01845-2601.

Lordy
Lordy

Look who's 40!

Look Who's 40

By Anita Wood
Cricut Cuts: Intermediate Level

MATERIALS

- Serenade Solutions Cartridge
- Songbird Cartridge
- Cardstock (black, pink, blue, green)
- Coordinating patterned paper (2 types with 1 striped)
- Adhesive
- Black gems

INSTRUCTIONS

Part 1: Cricut Die-Cut Pieces

Cartridge	Page #	Keypad #	Basic Key	Creative Feature Key	Shift	Function	Paper Type	Qty.	Size
Serenade Solutions	Pamphlet	49	Scroll 2		No		Black cardstock	2	3"
Serenade Solutions	Pamphlet	49	Scroll 2		No	Flip	Black cardstock	2	3"
Serenade Solutions	Pamphlet	36	Flamingo		No		Black cardstock	5	3½"
Serenade Solutions	Pamphlet	36	Flamingo		No	Flip	Black cardstock	5	3½"
Serenade Solutions	Pamphlet	36	Flamingo		No		Black cardstock	10	2½"
Serenade Solutions	Pamphlet	36	Flamingo		No	Flip	Black cardstock	10	2½"
Serenade Solutions	Pamphlet	36	Flamingo		No		Black cardstock	5	2"
Serenade Solutions	Pamphlet	36	Flamingo		No	Flip	Black cardstock	5	2"
Serenade Solutions	Pamphlet	36	Flamingo-s	Layer	No		Pink cardstock	5	3½"
Serenade Solutions	Pamphlet	36	Flamingo-s	Layer	No	Flip	Pink cardstock	5	3½"
Serenade Solutions	Pamphlet	36	Flamingo-s	Layer	No		Pink cardstock	10	2½"
Serenade Solutions	Pamphlet	36	Flamingo-s	Layer	No	Flip	Pink cardstock	10	2½"
Serenade Solutions	Pamphlet	36	Flamingo-s	Layer	No		Pink cardstock	10	2½"
Serenade Solutions	Pamphlet	36	Flamingo-s	Layer	No		Pink cardstock	5	2"
Serenade Solutions	Pamphlet	36	Flamingo-s	Layer	No		Pink cardstock	5	2"

Cartridge	Page #	Keypad #	Basic Key	Creative Feature Key	Shift	Function	Paper Type	Qty.	Size
Songbird	35, 38, 41, 27, 48	29, 19, 14, 23, 16	L, o, r, d, y		Yes on "L" only		Black cardstock	2 of each letter	2"
Songbird	35, 38, 34, 46, 31, 38, 42	29, 19, 18, 12, 26, 22	L, o, k, w, h, s		Yes on "L"		Black cardstock	1 of each letter, 3 o's	1¼"
Songbird	53, 59, 50	4, 10, 1	4, 0, !		Yes on "!" only		Black cardstock	1 of each character	2"
Songbird	61	38	Frame 1		No		Lime green cardstock	1	4¾"
Songbird	61	38	Frame 1		No		Aqua blue cardstock	1	4½"
Songbird	62	39	Frame 2		No		Lime green cardstock	1	4¼"
Songbird	62	39	Frame 2		No		Aqua blue cardstock	1	4"
Songbird	62	39	Frame 2		Yes		Lime green cardstock	1	4¾"
Songbird	62	39	Frame 2		Yes		Aqua blue cardstock	1	4½"

Part 2: Assembly

1. Cut two 12" x 2¼" pieces of striped patterned paper.

2. Adhere striped paper pieces horizontally to the center of each page.

3. Assemble frames, layering the blue over the green.

4. Adhere frames to the layout, as shown.

5. Adhere the lettering to layout, as shown.

6. Attach scrolls to the upper-right and lower-left corner of the left page of the layout.

7. Attach scrolls to the upper-left and lower-right corner of the right page of the layout.

8. Assemble flamingo die cuts, as shown.

9. Attach black crystal eyes to flamingos.

10. Adhere flamingos to the layout, as shown.

11. For added weight, attach finished layouts to white 12" x 12" cardstock.

YOU & ME

Birds of a Feather

By Cathie Rigby
Cricut Cuts: Intermediate Level

MATERIALS

- Straight from the Nest Cartridge
- Glue pen and other adhesive
- Black, silver, light blue, brown, jade, aqua cardstock
- Fine-tip black pen or marker
- Large brads
- Small sharp scissors
- Flowers and gems
- Raffia
- Brown loop ribbon
- Small-link silver chain
- Large-dot patterned paper (blue and cream)
- Bird image patterned paper
- Striped patterned paper
- Coordinating bird stamp set
- Silver loop fibers
- Jump ring

INSTRUCTIONS

Part 1: Cricut Die-Cut Pieces

Cartridge	Page #	Keypad #	Basic Key	Shift	Creative Feature Key	Paper Type	Qty.	Size
Straight from the Nest	35	8	Brdcg1-s	Yes		Black cardstock	1	3¾"
Straight from the Nest	35	8	Birdcge1			Silver cardstock	1	3¾"
Straight from the Nest	35	8	Birdcge1		Layer/Shadow	Light blue cardstock	1	3¾"
Straight from the Nest	35	8	Birdcge1	No	Corner	Brown cardstock	1	¾"
Straight from the Nest	55	28	Birdcge1	No	Phrase	Black cardstock	1	3½"
Straight from the Nest	55	28	Feathr-s	Yes	Phrase	Aqua cardstock	1	3½"

Tip: Keep all cut pieces on the mat until ready to assemble. This will give you an outline to follow when putting the phrase together.

Part 2: Assembly

1. Cut three 4" x 6" pieces from the large-dot patterned paper.

2. Cut one 5½" x 4" piece from the large-dot patterned paper.

3. Cut three 4¼" x 6¼" pieces from the jade cardstock.

4. Cut one 5¾" x 4¼" piece from the jade cardstock.

5. Glue large-dot patterned paper pieces to a piece of aqua cardstock to create photo mats.

6. Cut 2 striped patterned paper pieces to 4" x 12".

7. Adhere 1 striped patterned paper piece to the middle of each aqua cardstock piece to create background.

8. Adhere brown loop ribbon to the top of each striped patterned paper piece from step 6.

9. Fussy cut 2 decorative patterns from a bird-themed paper collection.

10. Adhere the fussy-cut images to the upper-left and lower-right corners of the layout, as shown, using dimensional adhesive.

11. Attach photo mats on the left page, as shown.

12. Add 4 or 5 coordinating flowers with gem centers to the lower-right corner of 1 photo mat.

13. Take a couple strands of raffia, fold in half, and glue under the flowers.

14. Assemble birdcage die cuts.

15. Add small-link silver chain to the top of the birdcage with a jump ring.

16. Adhere bird cage to upper-right corner and glue loose end of chain to the back side of the layout.

17. Adhere a coordinating die-cut sentiment to the right side of the layout with large brads.

18. Glue corner die-cut piece to photo mat on the left side of layout.

19. On the right page of the layout, stamp the upper-right and lower-left corners, as shown.

20. Adhere photo mats to the top half of the right page.

21. Repeat steps 10 and 11 on the smaller photo mat on the right page.

22. Adhere the title die-cut pieces to the right page.

23. Glue silver fiber just under the left corner of fussy-cut bird images on the right page.

short CIRCUIT

Short Circuit

By Cathie Rigby
Cricut Cuts: Advanced Level

MATERIALS

- Destinations Cartridge
- Plantin Schoolbook Cartridge
- Robotz Cartridge
- Robot 1 and Robot 2 Cartridges

- Glue pen and adhesive
- Cardstock
- Fine-tip black pen or marker
- Sharp small scissors

INSTRUCTIONS

Part 1: Cricut Die-Cut Pieces

Cartridge	Page #	Keypad #	Basic Key	Shift	Creative Feature Key	Mode	Paper Type	Qty.	Size
Destinations	74	47	KualLmpr	No	Sites	Portrait mode	Gray cardstock	1	11"
Plantin Schoolbook	69		City	No	Shadow	Fit to Length*	Aqua cardstock	1	11"
Plantin Schoolbook	69		City	No			Gray cardstock	1	3¼" or size your Cricut indicated on the previous cut in Fit to Length Mode**
Robotz	Various	22, 26, 19, 14, 15	Short	No	Font		Black cardstock	1 of each letter	1"
Robotz	Various	33, 18, 14 (press Flip key), 33, 17, 18, 15	CIRCUIT	Yes	Font	Mix 'n Match	Black cardstock	1 of each letter	1½"

*Note: Since you are using the Fit to Length Mode write down the height measurement for your next cut.

**Cutting tip: Cut large pieces on one mat and smaller pieces on a second mat.

Cartridge	Page #	Keypad #	Basic Key	Shift	Creative Feature Key	Paper Type	Qty.	Size
Robot 1								
Robotz	60	33	Robot33	No		Aqua cardstock	1	3½"
Robotz	60	33	Robot33-s	Yes		Black cardstock	1	3½"
Robotz	60	33	Robot33	No	Layer1	Lime green cardstock	1	3½"
Robotz	60	33	Robot33-s	Yes	Layer1	Black cardstock	1	3½"
Robotz	60	33	Robot33	No	Layer2/Shadow	White cardstock	1	3½"
Robotz	60	33	Robot33-s	Yes	Layer2/Shadow	Purple cardstock	1	3½"***

*** Assembling tip: Leave smaller pieces on the mat until ready to assemble. If a piece is lost or did not cut correctly, use a piece from the extra images cut. This speeds up assembly process and prevents re-cuts in the middle of a project.

Cartridge	Page #	Keypad #	Basic Key	Shift	Creative Feature Key	Paper Type	Qty.	Size
Robot 2								
Robotz	60	3	Robot33-s	Yes	Layer2/Shadow	Purple cardstock	1	$3\frac{1}{2}$"
Robotz	71	44	Robot44-s	Yes	Font	Gray cardstock	1	1"
Robotz	71	44	Robot44-s	Yes	Font	Gray cardstock	1	$1\frac{3}{4}$"
Robotz	71	44	Robot44-s	Yes	Font	Gray cardstock	1	2"
Robotz	71	44	Robot44	No	Font	Aqua cardstock	1	$1\frac{3}{4}$"
Robotz	71	44	Robot44	No	Font	Aqua cardstock	1	2"
Robotz	71	44	Robot44	No	Font Shadow	Gray cardstock	1	$1\frac{3}{4}$"
Robotz	71	44	Robot44	No	Font Shadow	Gray cardstock	1	2"
Robotz	71	44	Robot44	No	Font Shadow	Gray cardstock	1	$1\frac{3}{4}$"

Note: You can create additional robots with layers. The pictured example has 4 robots and uses the following for the extra 2:
Page 57 Button #30, Robot30 Size $3\frac{1}{2}$" with all layers
Page 67 Button #40, Robot40 Size 4" with all layers

Part 2: Assembly

1. Assemble all robot die cuts, according to the image shown.

2. Cut 2 strips of $1\frac{1}{2}$" x $11\frac{3}{4}$" grid patterned paper.

3. Cut two $1\frac{3}{4}$" x 12" strips of dark gray cardstock.

4. Adhere grid paper to gray cardstock strips.

5. Attach both strips from step 3 to the bottom of two 12" x 12" pieces of tan cardstock.

6. Cut two $4\frac{1}{4}$" x $6\frac{1}{4}$" circuit-patterned paper pieces.

7. Cut two $4\frac{1}{2}$" x $6\frac{1}{2}$" pieces of purple cardstock.

8. Adhere circuit patterned paper to purple cardstock pieces, and attach to right side of layout.

9. Adhere gray city die-cut piece to the aqua shadow piece, and attach to right side of layout, as shown.

10. Adhere 2 different robot die cuts to the bottom edges of the right side of layout.

11. Adhere with dimensional adhesive a third robot die-cut in between the 2 robots on the right side of the layout.

12. Adhere screw die-cut shapes to upper-right corner of layout.

13. Cut four $3\frac{1}{2}$" x $3\frac{1}{2}$" squares of circuit patterned paper.

14. Cut 1 square of purple cardstock to $7\frac{1}{2}$" x $7\frac{1}{2}$".

15. Cut the square from step 14 into 4 equal squares to create mats.

16. Adhere patterned paper squares on top of the purple cardstock squares.

17. Adhere all squares to the left page of the layout, as shown.

18. Adhere the building die cut to the left page of layout, as shown.

19. Adhere the last robot to the base of the building.

20. Adhere the sprocket-shaped die cut to the center of the squares from step 16 with dimensional adhesive.

21. Adhere the title to left side of the layout.

Winter Wonderland

By Cathie Rigby
Cricut Cuts: Advanced Level

MATERIALS

- Winter Frolic Cartridge
- Simply Charmed Cartridge
- Winter Woodland Cartridge

- Glue Pen
- Liquid adhesive
- Dimensional adhesive
- Cardstock (red, aqua, olive green, black, and white)
- Snowflake patterned paper
- Fine-tip black pen or marker
- Cricut deep-cut blade and housing
- White craft foam sheet
- Sharp small scissors
- Glass glitter or white glitter
- Spiderweb embossing folder
- Cuttlebug
- Buttons
- Craft thread
- White inkpad
- Corner rounder punch

Winter Wonderland

INSTRUCTIONS

Part 1: Cricut Die-Cut Pieces

Cartridge	Page #	Keypad #	Basic Key	Shift	Creative Feature Key	Mode	Paper Type	Qty.	Size
Winter Frolic	54	27	NorthPol	No			Green cardstock	1	6¼"
Winter Frolic	54	27	NorthPol	Yes			White cardstock	1	6¼"
Winter Frolic	54	27	NorthPol	No	Layer		Aqua cardstock	1	6¼"
Winter Frolic	54	27	NorthPol	Yes	Layer		Brown cardstock	1	6¼"
Winter Frolic	54	27	NorthPol	Yes	Layer		Red cardstock	1	6¼"
Winter Frolic	54	27	NorthPol	Yes	Border		Green cardstock	2	6¼"
Winter Frolic	66	39	Presents	No	Border	Fit to Length	White cardstock	1	11½"
Winter Frolic	66	39	Presents	No	Border		White cardstock	2	1½"
Winter Frolic	40	13	Girl2	Yes	Phrase	Fit to Length	Black cardstock	1	7"

Note: You will discard "Winter" portion.

Cartridge	Page #	Keypad #	Basic Key	Shift	Creative Feature Key	Mode	Paper Type	Qty.	Size
Winter Frolic	40	13	Girl2	No	Phrase	Fit to Length	Aqua cardstock	1	5½"
Winter Frolic	40	13	Girl2	Yes	Phrase		Black cardstock	1	2½"
Winter Frolic	28	1	Snowman1	Yes	Phrase		White craft foam sheet*	1	3"
Simply Charmed	66	39	Penguin2	Yes			Black cardstock	1	3"
Simply Charmed	66	39	Penguin2	Yes	Layer1		White cardstock	1	3"
Simply Charmed	66	39	Penguin2	Yes	Layer2		Orange cardstock	1	3"
Simply Charmed	66	39	Penguin2	Yes	Layer3		Pink cardstock	1	3"
Simply Charmed	66	39	Penguin2	Yes	Layer4		Aqua cardstock	1	3"
Winter Woodland	48	17	Cap	No			Aqua patterned paper	1	2"
Winter Woodland	48	17	Cap	No	Layers		White cardstock	1	2"
Simply Charmed	66	39	Penguin1	No			Black cardstock	1	3"
Simply Charmed	66	39	Penguin1	No	Layer1		White cardstock	1	3"
Simply Charmed	66	39	Penguin1	No	Layer2		Orange cardstock	1	3"
Simply Charmed	66	39	Penguin1	No	Layer3		Red cardstock	1	3"

*Use the deep-cut blade settings: speed 3, pressure 4, blade 4.

Part 2: Assembly

1. Assemble penguin die cuts, as shown.

2. Assemble North Pole sign die cuts, as shown.

3. With a Cuttlebug, emboss larger tree pieces with the Spiderweb embossing folder.

Note: If you don't own a Cuttlebug, you can create the same dimension by folding the trees to create similar creases.

4. Ink the ridges and edges of the trees with a white inkpad.

5. Use 2 pieces of 12" x 12" snowflake patterned paper for base of layout.

6. Cut 2 strips of white cardstock measuring 2½" x 12".

7. Adhere white strips to the bottom of both base pages.

8. Cut a 5" x 7" piece and two 2" x 2" squares of red cardstock.

9. Use a corner rounder punch to round all corners of red cardstock.

10. Adhere to the right side of layout, as shown.

11. Cut a 5" x 5" piece and a 4" x 6" piece of red cardstock.

12. Use a corner rounder punch to round all corners of red cardstock.

13. Adhere pieces to the left side of layout, as shown.

14. Adhere North Pole die cut just under the 4" x 6" photo mat.

15. Adhere smaller snowflake flourishes to both photo mats on the left page.

16. Thread craft thread through 2 buttons for the centers of 2 snowflakes.

17. Adhere the buttons to the center of the large flower on each flourish.

18. Add title die cuts to top of the 5" x 5" photo mat.

19. Adhere the larger snowflake flourish to right side of layout.

20. Add thread to a button and adhere it to center of the large flower on flourish.

21. Add tree die cuts along the bottom of page on the right side of layout.

22. Adhere penguins to the layout using dimensional adhesive.

23. Use a liquid adhesive to add highlights of glass glitter or white glitter along the bottom of layout and on all of the flourishes to simulate snow crystals.

24. Adhere foam snowflake to the center of large snowflake on the flourish.

25. Add glass glitter or white glitter to the foam snowflake for dimension.

remembering

cool memories

boys rule!

GROWING

This was so cute!

xxx

WE couldn't stop laughing because...

Growing

By Cathie Rigby
Cricut Cuts: Advanced Level

MATERIALS

- Carousel Cartridge
- Freshly Picked Cartridge
- New Arrival Cartridge
- Plantin Schoolbook Cartridge
- Accent Essentials Cartridge
- Nursery Rhyme Cartridge
- Paisley Cartridge
- Adhesive
- Dimensional adhesive
- Cardstock (dark brown, white, light turquoise, dark turquoise, dark green, olive, blue, light brown, light green)
- Patterned paper (wood grain, leaves, combination motif)
- Journaling cards
- Pom-pom trim
- Brown and pink markers
- White gel pen
- Twine
- Green silk ribbon
- Photo turn
- Mini brads

INSTRUCTIONS

Part 1: Cricut Die-Cut Pieces

Cartridge	Page #	Keypad #	Basic Key	Shift	Creative Feature Key	Function	Paper Type	Qty.	Size
Plantin Schoolbook	38		G	Yes			Dark brown cardstock	2	2"
Plantin Schoolbook	54		W	Yes			Dark brown cardstock	1	1.6"
Plantin Schoolbook	45		N	Yes			Dark brown cardstock	1	1.7"
Plantin Schoolbook	38		G	Yes			Dark brown cardstock	1	1.8"
Carousel	Pamphlet	19	O	Yes	Font		Dark brown cardstock	1	2"
Carousel	Pamphlet	18	I	Yes	Font		Dark brown cardstock	1	1.7"
Nursery Rhyme	37	14	JckJill-s	Yes	Font		Dark brown cardstock	1	2.25"
Paisley	24	1	Snail-s	Yes			Dark turquoise cardstock	1	1.5"
Paisley	24	1	Snail-s	Yes	Layer1		Light brown cardstock	1	1.5"
Paisley	24	1	Snail-s	Yes		Flip	Dark turquoise cardstock	1	1"
Paisley	24	1	Snail-s	Yes	Layer1	Flip	Light brown cardstock	1	1"

Cartridge	Page #	Keypad #	Basic Key	Shift	Creative Feature Key	Function	Paper Type	Qty.	Size
Freshly Picked	34	7	Mushroom	No			Light brown cardstock	1	1.60"
Freshly Picked	34	7	Mushroom	No			Dark turquoise cardstock	1	1.6"
Freshly Picked	34	7	Mshrm-s	Yes			Light brown cardstock	1	3"
Freshly Picked	34	7	Mshrm-s	Yes			Dark turquoise cardstock	1	3"
Freshly Picked	34	7	Mshrm-s	Yes		Flip	Light brown cardstock	1	2"
Freshly Picked	34	7	Mshrm-s	Yes		Flip	Dark turquoise cardstock	1	2"
Accent Essentials	72	41	Accent41	No		Flip	Dark brown cardstock	1	2"
Accent Essentials	72	41	Accent41	No			Dark brown cardstock	1	2"
New Arrival	116	35	Frog	No			Olive green cardstock	1	3"
New Arrival	116	35	Frog	Yes			Mint green cardstock	1	3"
New Arrival	116	35	Frog	No	Blackout		White cardstock	1	3"

Part 2: Assembly

Left Page

1. Use 2 green 12" x 12" cardstock pieces as layout base pages.

2. Use patterned paper with blue dot and woodgrain frame, and cut out the inside portion of frame.

3. Adhere frame patterned paper to green cardstock base.

4. Cut 1 light turquoise cardstock piece measuring 4¼" x 6¼" and ink the edges with brown ink.

5. Cut 1 light turquoise cardstock piece to 3¼" x 5" and ink the edges with brown ink.

6. Mat 2 journaling cards with dark brown cardstock and turquoise cardstock.

7. Attach 4 small brads to the larger journaling card, and adhere the card to the upper right of page.

8. Adhere the 4¼" x 6¼" photo mat to the lower right of page.

9. Adhere the 4½" x 5" photo mat to the upper-left side of page.

10. Fussy cut an animal image from the patterned paper (or use a sticker), and adhere to the page above the smaller photo mat using dimensional adhesive, as shown.

11. Attach the photo turn under the smaller photo mat, as shown.

12. Adhere die-cut letters across center of the page, as shown.

Note: O and I letters have been turned upside down.

13. Take large and small single mushrooms and cut off the stems from the dark turquoise pieces.

14. Add detail marks on the turquoise pieces, as shown.

15. Add coordinating pom-pom trim to the larger brown mushroom die cut.

16. Adhere turquoise tops to the mushrooms.

Note: Use dimensional adhesive on the larger mushroom.

17. Slide journaling block under larger mushroom.

Right Page

1. Cut strip of patterned paper to 2" x 12".

Note: Use a craft knife to create a curved edge, as shown.

2. Cut leaf patterned paper to 4¼" x 12", and adhere to the right of center on the green cardstock base, as shown.

3. Cut a 2" x 12" dark brown cardstock piece, and adhere it to the left of the leaf patterned paper.

4. Adhere curved patterned paper to the left of dark brown cardstock piece.

5. Place a small strip of adhesive along the seam of the patterned paper and dark brown cardstock.

6. Attach the green silk ribbon on the strip of adhesive, creating ruffles as you go.

7. Adhere the ends of ribbon to the back of the page.

8. Cut 1 light turquoise cardstock piece measuring 4¼" x 6¼" and ink the edges with brown ink.

9. Cut 1 light turquoise cardstock piece to 4½" x 5" and ink the edges with brown ink.

10. Wrap twine around the large photo mat and adhere to the right side of page.

11. Place the smaller photo mat on the lower right of the page.

12. Cut a scrap piece of light brown cardstock to create a photo corner and adhere to bottom of the page.

13. Place die-cut leaves along the left edge of page.

14. Assemble frog die cut and use a brown marker to draw the mouth and eyes of the frog.

15. Place the frog on the oval, and adhere it to the page next to the leaves, as shown.

16. Attach the journaling block under leaves and frog, as shown.

17. Cut the stems off the dark turquoise mushrooms.

18. Adhere pom-pom trim to the larger mushroom top.

19. Adhere turquoise tops to the light brown mushroom pieces.

Note: Use dimensional adhesive on the larger mushroom.

20. Adhere finished mushrooms to the lower-left side of page.

21. Assemble snail die cuts and use markers to add accents, as shown.

22. Adhere snails to the corner of the photo mats, as shown.

We're not perfect We're ✦FAMILY

We're Family

By Anita Wood
Cricut Cuts: Advanced Level

MATERIALS

- Stone Script Solutions Cartridge
- Heritage Cartridge
- Simply Charmed Cartridge
- Cardstock (light brown, dark brown, white, light blue, yellow green, lime green)
- Patterned paper (coordinating green, brown, and blue patterns)

- Brown inkpad
- Thread
- Sewing machine
- Brown sheer ribbon

INSTRUCTIONS

Part 1: Preparation

1. Tear 7 strips of coordinating patterned paper in varying widths for the page background.

2. Ink the edges of each torn strip.

Part 2: Cricut Die-Cut Pieces

Cartridge	Page #	Keypad #	Basic Key	Shift	Creative Feature Key	Paper Type	Qty.	Size
Stone Script Solutions	Pamphlet		w, e, ', r, n, o, t, p, f, c	Yes on w		Dark brown cardstock	2 (w, ', t), 6 (e), 3 (r), 1 (n, o, p, f, c)	1¼"
Heritage	39	16	House6	Yes	Word	Brown cardstock	1	1½"
Heritage	24	1	Tree1	No		Light brown cardstock	1	6¼"
Heritage	24	1	Tree1	No	Shadow	Dark brown cardstock	1	6¼"
Heritage	24	1	Leaves1	Yes	Shadow	Yellow green cardstock	3	1½"
Heritage	24	1	Leaves1	Yes	Shadow	Lime green cardstock	3	1½"
Heritage	24	1	Leaves1	Yes	Shadow	Yellow green cardstock	3	1¼"
Heritage	24	1	Leaves1	Yes	Shadow	Lime green cardstock	3	1¼"
Heritage	25	2	Leaves2	Yes	Shadow	Lime green cardstock	2	1½"
Heritage	25	2	Leaves2	Yes	Shadow	Yellow green cardstock	2	1½"
Heritage	35	12	Church2	Yes	Charm	White cardstock	1	4"
Heritage	35	12	Church2	No	Charm	Light blue cardstock	1	4"
Heritage	45	22	Fence3	Yes	Charm	White cardstock	1	4"
Heritage	45	22	Fence3	Yes	Charm	Lime green cardstock	1	4"
Heritage	33	10	Barn	Yes	Charm	White cardstock	1	4"
Heritage	33	10	Barn	No	Charm	Lime green cardstock	1	4"
Heritage	63	40	Bike2	Yes	Charm	White cardstock	1	3½"
Heritage	63	40	Bike2	No	Charm	Light blue cardstock	1	3½"
Simply Charmed	69	42		No	Layer 3	White cardstock	1	2½"
Simply Charmed	69	42		No	Layer 3	White cardstock	2	1¾"
Simply Charmed	69	42	Rainbow	No	Layer 3	Light blue cardstock	2	1¾"
Simply Charmed	69	42	Rainbow	No	Layer 3	Light blue cardstock	2	2"

Part 3: Assembly

1. Use 12" x 12" brown cardstock to create the page base.

2. Layer the background strips from top to bottom, as shown.

Note: Overlap each layer so all seven strips fill the entire 12" x 12" page.

3. Attach each strip of paper with a little bit of adhesive.

4. Zig-zag stitch around the entire page with a sewing machine.

5. Single stitch each strip of paper at top, torn edge.

6. Layer the tree base on the shadow.

7. With a brown ink pad, lightly stamp ink on the tree in a sponge/stippling effect.

8. Lightly ink the edges of each colored frame.

9. Layer each frame on coordinating white base.

10. Adhere the clouds, lettering, tree, and frames to the page, as shown.

11. Attach the leaves to the tree and below the tree, as shown.

12. Adhere a knotted piece of sheer ribbon to top of each frame.

Captured Flight

Kitchen Secrets

Forever Love

Sew Organized

Smile Banner

Illuminating Elegance

Mon Amour

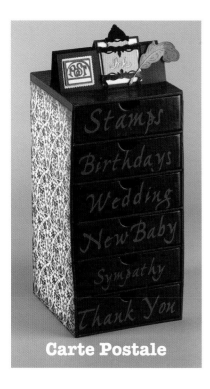

Carte Postale

Memories

Seasonal Charm

Inspire Me

Bless This Home

Warm Winter Wishes

Autumn Glow

Under the Big Top

Springtime Happiness

Captured Flight

By Gabriela Villaseñor
Cricut Cuts: Beginner Level

MATERIALS

- Serenade Cartridge
- White Cardstock
- Gray Cardstock
- Fine and coarse glitter
- Scoring board and scoring tool
- Paper trimmer
- Tacky tape adhesive
- Normal adhesive
- Dimensional adhesive
- Thread
- Sheer silver ribbon
- Metal butterfly embellishment

INSTRUCTIONS

Part 1: Cricut Die-Cut Pieces

Cartridge	Page #	Keypad #	Basic Key	Shift	Paper Type	Qty.	Size
Serenade	Pamphlet	42	Birdcage2	No	White cardstock	4	5½"
Serenade	Pamphlet	11	Butterfly3	No	White cardstock	1	2¼"
Serenade	Pamphlet	11	Butterfly3	Yes	Gray cardstock	1	2¼"

Part 2: Assembly

1. Cut a 3½" square of white cardstock.

2. Score the square at ¼" on each side with a scoring board and tool.

3. Adhere the 4 birdcage panels to each other using tacky tape.

4. Adhere the bottom square to the birdcage panels.

5. Use thread to attach the metal butterfly attachment to the birdcage.

6. Use thread again to attach the 4 tops of the cage panels.

7. Make a bow from the silver ribbon and attach to the top of the birdcage.

8. Use adhesive to assemble butterfly cuts.

9. Add fine glitter to the larger base piece of the butterfly.

10. Add coarse glitter to the smaller layer of butterfly.

11. Attach the butterfly with dimensional adhesive to the top of birdcage.

Kitchen Secrets

By Paula Sanders
Cricut Cuts: Beginner Level

MATERIALS

- From My Kitchen Cartridge
- Cardstock (blue, green, white, red)
- Patterned paper with blue, red, green, and white (2 coordinating patterns)
- Tin recipe box (5" x 7" x 4")
- Ribbon (red, green)
- Adhesive

INSTRUCTIONS

Part 1: Cricut Die-Cut Pieces for Cover

Cartridge	Page #	Keypad #	Basic Key	Shift	Creative Feature Key	Paper Type	Qty.	Size
From My Kitchen	69	42	Spghti	No	Tabs	Cardstock	4	4"
From My Kitchen	68	41	Plater	No	Tabs	Cardstock	4	4"
From My Kitchen	70	43	Lobstr	No	Tabs	Cardstock	4	4"
From My Kitchen	69	42	Spghti	No	Ovals	Cardstock	1	½"
From My Kitchen	69	42	Spghti	No	Ovals Shadow	Cardstock	1	½"
From My Kitchen	73	46	Meat	No	Ovals	Cardstock	1	½"
From My Kitchen	73	46	Meat	No	Ovals Shadow	Cardstock	1	½"
From My Kitchen	67	40	Pie	No	Ovals	Cardstock	1	½"
From My Kitchen	67	40	Pie	No	Ovals Shadow	Cardstock	1	½"
From My Kitchen	66	39	Eggs	No	Ovals	Cardstock	1	½"
From My Kitchen	66	39	Eggs	No	Ovals Shadow	Cardstock	1	½"
From My Kitchen	64	37	Bread	No	Ovals	Cardstock	1	½"
From My Kitchen	64	37	Bread	No	Ovals Shadow	Cardstock	1	½"
From My Kitchen	65	38	Cookies	No	Ovals	Cardstock	1	½"
From My Kitchen	65	38	Cookies	No	Ovals Shadow	Cardstock	1	½"
From My Kitchen	63	36	Cake	No	Ovals	Cardstock	1	½"
From My Kitchen	63	36	Cake	No	Ovals Shadow	Cardstock	1	½"
From My Kitchen	61	34	Cpcake	No	Ovals	Cardstock	1	½"
From My Kitchen	61	34	Cpcake	No	Ovals Shadow	Cardstock	1	½"
From My Kitchen	43	16	Spoon-s	Yes	Ovals	Green cardstock	1	2"
From My Kitchen	43	16	Spoon-s	Yes	Ovals Shadow	Blue cardstock	1	2"
From My Kitchen	43	16	Spoon-s	Yes	Ovals Shadow	White cardstock	1	2¼"
From My Kitchen	58	41	Sltppr	No		Green cardstock	1	2"
From My Kitchen	58	41	Sltppr-s	Yes		White cardstock	1	2"
From My Kitchen	36	9	Pot	No		Red cardstock	1	2"
From My Kitchen	36	9	Pot-s	Yes		Blue cardstock	1	2"
From My Kitchen	36	9	Pot-s	No	Layers	White cardstock	1	2"

Part 2: Assembly

1. Adhere each food item to its coordinating oval background piece.

2. Adhere each assembled food piece to a divider card.

Note: There will be a few extra divider cards, in case you choose to do extra cards or mess up on a card.

3. Cut 2 $4\frac{1}{4}$" x 10" pieces of patterned paper and adhere around the outside of the tin box.

4. Place tin box on top of second patterned paper and trace.

5. Cut out the traced portion.

6. Place cut paper on the lid, and trace where the handles are and cut out handle areas.

7. Adhere cut paper to the lid of the tin box.

8. Assemble salt and pepper shaker pieces.

9. Adhere salt and pepper shakers to one side of the tin box.

10. Assemble the pot pieces.

11. Adhere the pot to the other side of the tin box.

12. Assemble the "recipes" sign.

13. Staple red ribbon to the "recipes" sign.

14. Adhere the "recipes" sign to the front of the tin box.

15. Adhere green ribbon around the bottom and top of the tin box.

16. Adhere red ribbon around the lid of the tin box.

Part 3: Die-Cut Pieces for Recipe Cards

Recipe cards for the inside of the tin can be customized for your particular needs. Included here are the cuts to create the fish and pasta tabs pictured.

Cartridge	Page #	Keypad #	Basic Key	Shift	Creative Feature Key	Paper Type	Qty.	Size
From My Kitchen	28	1	Phone	No	Tabs	Blue cardstock	3	5"
From My Kitchen	68	41	Plater	No		Blue cardstock	1	1½"
From My Kitchen	68	41	Plater	Yes	Layers	White cardstock	1	2¼"
From My Kitchen	68	41	Plater	No	Shadow/Blackout	Dark Red cardstock	1	1½"
From My Kitchen	68	41	Plater	Yes	Shadow/Blackout	Red cardstock	1	1½"
From My Kitchen	68	41	Plater	No	Words	White vinyl	1	¼"
From My Kitchen	68	42	Spghti	No		White cardstock	1	2"
From My Kitchen	69	42	Spghti	Yes	Layers	Red cardstock	1	2"
From My Kitchen	69	42	Spghti	No	Shadow/Blackout	Red cardstock	1	2"
From My Kitchen	69	42	Spghti	No	Words	White vinyl	1	¼"

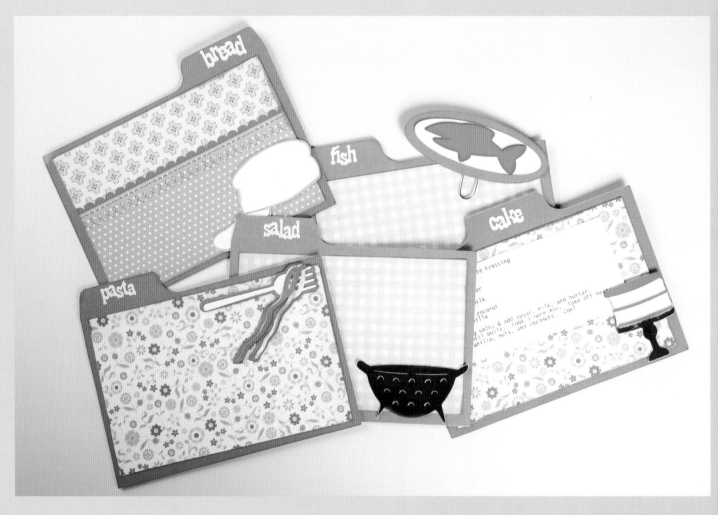

Forever Love

By Cathie Rigby
Cricut Cuts: Beginner Level

MATERIALS

- Elegant Cakes Cartridge
- Mother's Day Bouquet Cartridge
- Acrylic block (4" x 3")
- Vinyl (red and black)
- Transfer tape
- Rhinestones
- Cardstock (red)
- Red sheer ribbon

INSTRUCTIONS

Part 1: Cricut Die-Cut Pieces

Cartridge	Page #	Keypad #	Basic Key	Creative Feature Key	Shift	Paper Type	Qty.	Size
Elegant Cakes	51, 46, 41, 40, 61, 40, 41	24, 19, 14, 13, 34, 13, 14	F, o, r, e, v, e, r	Plain Font	Yes on F	Black vinyl	1	.80"
Base Camp	103, 106, 113, 96		L, O, V, E	Font	Yes on all letters	Red vinyl	1	1¼"

Part 2: Assembly

1. Cut red cardstock to 3½" x 2½".

2. Adhere 3" x 2" photo to cardstock.

3. Adhere to back of acrylic block so the photo shows through.

4. Use transfer tape to pick up and place the red vinyl letters at the bottom of the front of block.

Note: For tips on working with vinyl, see page 28.

5. Use transfer tape to pick up and place black vinyl letters over top of the red vinyl letters.

6. Adhere rhinestones to the four corners of the block.

Sew Organized

By Cathie Rigby
Cricut Cuts: Beginner Level

MATERIALS

- Accent Essentials Cartridge
- Wall Décor and More Cartridge
- Ashlyn's Alphabet Cartridge
- Happily Ever After Cartridge
- Adhesive
- Sewing-themed patterned paper (red flower, blue flower, tape measure, stitched design)
- Cardstock (red, dark pink, light pink, turquoise, green, black, craft, silver, yellow)
- Clear dimensional glaze
- Brown feathers
- White feather boa
- Set of 3 canisters
- Eyelets
- Flowers (brown suede)
- String pearl trim
- Self-adhesive pearls
- White trim
- Mini buttons
- Green mulberry paper
- Inkpad
- Hot glue gun

INSTRUCTIONS

Part 1: Cricut Die-Cut Pieces

Cartridge	Page #	Keypad #	Basic Key	Shift	Creative Feature Key	Paper Type	Qty.	Size
Accent Essentials	79	48	Accnt48s	Yes		Red cardstock	1	4"
Accent Essentials	79	48	Accent48	No		Flower patterned paper	1	4"
Accent Essentials	79	48	Accnt48s	Yes		Dark pink cardstock	1	3"
Accent Essentials	79	48	Accent48	No		Stitched patterned paper	1	3"
Accent Essentials	79	48	Accnt48s	Yes		Turquoise cardstock	1	2"
Accent Essentials	79	48	Accent48	No		Blue flower patterned paper	1	2"
Wall Décor and More	74	47	DrsForm	No		Green cardstock, black cardstock	2 (1 of each color)	4"
Wall Décor and More	74	47	DrsForm-s	Yes		Pink cardstock	1	4"
Wall Décor and More	70	43	Scissor	No		Green cardstock	1	3"
Wall Décor and More	70	43	Scisor-s	Yes		Black cardstock	1	3"
Ashlyn's Alphabet	66	39	Heart	No	Icon	Pink cardstock	1	6"
Happily Ever After	35	8	JaqGus	No	Icon	Craft cardstock, silver cardstock	2 (1 of each)	1¾"
Happily Ever After	35	8	JaqGus	Yes	Icon	Yellow cardstock	1	1¾"

Part 2: Assembly

Large Canister

1. Adhere measuring tape paper around the canister. Have the edges end towards the front of canister.

2. Take the square-shaped tag die cuts and punch each corner with a scallop punch to create indentations in all of the corners.

3. Adhere patterned paper die cuts to the center of the cardstock companion piece.

4. Adhere the tag to the front of the canister over the seam edges of measuring tape strips.

5. Attach a self-adhesive pearl flourish to the left side of tag.

6. Adhere a couple of brown feathers and a brown suede flower to the left side of tag.

7. Adhere a 1/2" piece of white boa feathers to the right side of tag.

Note: Leave enough room in the center of the tag to adhere the center pieces.

8. Cut off the top portion of the black dress form die cut and adhere to the top of the green dress form piece.

9. Adhere assembled green dress form to the pink dress form piece.

10. Adhere dress form to the center of the pink oval die cut.

11. Attach strand of white pearls along the edge of the pink oval piece using a clear-drying adhesive.

12. With dimensional adhesive, attach the pink oval piece to the center of tag on the canister, and tuck some of the brown feathers behind the oval.

13. Attach white trim around the lid of canister with hot glue.

Medium Canister

1. Adhere measuring tape paper around the canister. Have the edges end towards the front of canister.

2. Take the square-shaped tag die cuts and punch each corner with a scallop punch to create indentations in all the corners.

3. Adhere patterned paper die cuts to the center of the cardstock companion piece.

4. Attach 4 small gold eyelets to each corner of tag shape.

5. Adhere the tag to the front of the canister over the seam edges of measuring tape strips.

6. Adhere a medium-sized cream silk flower and small cream feathers to the center of the tag.

7. Adhere green scissor die-cut piece onto the black shadow scissor piece.

Note: Do not remove the black cardstock from the inside of scissor holes. These can be taped on the back to keep in place.

8. Attach a small black brad to the center of the scissors.

9. Use a clear dimensional glaze over the scissors image to create a shiny finish.

10. When the scissors piece is completely dry, adhere to the center of the cream flower.

Note: Make sure the feathers show from underneath scissors piece.

11. Use hot glue to attach white trim around the lid of canister.

Small Canister

1. Adhere measuring tape paper around the canister. Have the edges end towards the front of canister.

2. Take the square-shaped tag die cuts and punch each corner with a scallop punch to create indentations in all the corners.

3. Adhere patterned paper die cuts to the center of the cardstock companion piece.

4. Adhere the tag to the front of the canister over the seam edges of measuring tape strips.

5. Cut a 3" x 2" piece of green mulberry paper.

6. Gently tear around all edges of the mulberry paper to create a fuzzy backing.

7. Adhere the mulberry paper to the center of the canister using a small amount of clear adhesive in the center.

8. Ink the edges of the spool die cut

9. Assemble the spool die cut with the yellow layer on top.

10. Cut off the silver needle from the die cut shape, and attach the needle over yellow piece.

11. Adhere assembled spool die cut to the center of the canister.

12. Adhere the tiny buttons to the lower right of the tag, just under the spool of thread.

13. Use hot glue to attach white trim around the lid of canister.

Smile Banner

By Katrina Hunt
Cricut Cuts: Beginner Level

MATERIALS

- Cindy Loo Cartridge
- Kate's ABC Cartridge
- Straight from the Nest Cartridge
- Patterned paper (pink, blue, yellow, yellow dot, green)
- Cardstock (brown)
- 6" x 6" chipboard album
- Baker's twine (pink)
- White button
- Pink and blue gems
- Adhesive
- Blue paint
- Cream mist paint
- Glitter pen
- Lace
- Inkpad (coordinating colors)
- Rainbow, camera, dragonfly paper images
- Sewing machine

INSTRUCTIONS

Part 1: Preparation

1. Cover chipboard album pieces with blue paint.

2. Mist each chipboard piece with cream mist and let dry.

Part 2: Cricut Die-Cut Pieces

Cartridge	Page #	Keypad #	Basic Key	Shift	Creative Feature Key	Paper Type	Qty.	Size
Owl								
Cindy Loo	60	33	Owl	No		Brown cardstock	1	2¾"
Cindy Loo	60	33	Owl-s	Yes		Pink patterned paper	1	2¾"
Cindy Loo	60	33	Owl	No	Layer	Yellow patterned paper	1	2¾"
Cindy Loo	60	33	Owl-s	Yes	Layer	Blue cardstock	1	2¾"
Smile								
Kate's ABCs	42	22	Shoes2	No	Baby Girl Font 2	Blue patterned paper	1	1¼"
Kate's ABCs	42	22	Shoes2-s	Yes	Baby Girl Font 2, Shadow	Green patterned paper	1	1¼"
Kate's ABCs	57	37	Mushroom	No	Baby Girl Font 2	Blue patterned paper	1	1¼"
Kate's ABCs	57	37	Mushrm-s	Yes	Baby Girl Font 2, Shadow	Green patterned paper	1	1¼"
Kate's ABCs	38	18	Sundae	No	Baby Girl Font 2	Blue patterned paper	1	1¼"
Kate's ABCs	38	18	Sundae-s	Yes	Baby Girl Font 2, Shadow	Green patterned paper	1	1¼"
Kate's ABCs	49	29	Ladybug	No	Baby Girl Font 2	Blue patterned paper	1	1¼"
Kate's ABCs	49	29	Ladybug-s	Yes	Baby Girl Font 2, Shadow	Green patterned paper	1	1¼"
Kate's ABCs	33	13	Bird	No	Baby Girl Font 2	Blue patterned paper	1	1¼"
Kate's ABCs	33	13	Bird-s	Yes	Baby Girl Font 2, Shadow	Green patterned paper	1	1¼"
Butterfly								
Kate's ABCs	62	42	Trike	No	Baby Girl Font 2	Brown cardstock	1	2¾"
Kate's ABCs	62	42	Trike-s	Yes	Baby Girl Font 2	Yellow patterned paper	1	2¾"
Kate's ABCs	62	42	Trike	No	Baby Girl Font 2, Shadow	Pink patterned paper	1	2¾"
Banner								
Straight from the Nest	39	12	Tree2	No	Border	Green patterned paper	25	1"
Straight from the Nest	65	38	Banner	No		Yellow dot patterned paper	5	5"
Straight from the Nest	65	38	Banner-s	Yes		Pink patterned paper	5	5"
Straight from the Nest	65	38	Banner-s	Yes		Green patterned paper	5	5"

Part 3: Assembly

1. Ink die-cut pieces, as desired.

Note: You do not need to ink every piece.

2. Attach the green border pieces to each side of the main yellow banner shape and make them meet at the point.

Note: You may have to trim or cut apart to get this to work out.

3. Machine stitch around each yellow dot portion of the banner.

4. Wrap twine around each pink top banner piece and attach to the identical green top banner pieces with dimensional adhesive.

Note: Offset the pieces so you can see the green piece underneath the pink, as shown.

5. After you get all the tops created, attach them to your banner pieces.

6. Attach completed pendant banner pieces to the chipboard pieces.

7. Layer "smile" letters on top of green shadows.

8. Attach the letters to the top of the pendant banner shapes.

9. Adhere a button for the dot on the "i."

10. Assemble owl.

11. Add gems for the eyes, and add the owl to the "l" chipboard.

12. Assemble the butterfly.

Note: Use dimensional adhesive for the top layer of the wings.

13. Add a border to the top wings with a glitter pen.

14. Attach gems to the wings and antennas of the butterfly.

15. Add the butterfly to the "m" chipboard.

16. Add the rainbow paper image to the "s" chipboard.

17. Add the camera paper image to the "i" chipboard.

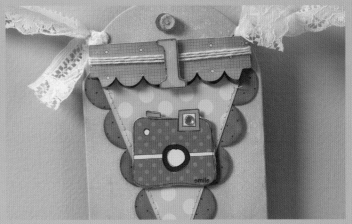

18. Add the dragonfly paper image to the "e" chipboard.

19. Adhere lace at the bottom of each chipboard piece.

20. Punch holes on the side of each chipboard piece.

21. String chipboard pieces together with lace.

Illuminating Elegance

By Lisa Sheffield
Cricut Cuts: Intermediate Level

MATERIALS

- Home Accents Cartridge
- Winter Woodland Cartridge
- Brown lamp with square-shaped lampshade
- 2 sheets brown cardstock, size 12" x 12"
- Clear glaze spray
- Hanging jewel decorations
- Adhesive that works on fabric

INSTRUCTIONS

Part 1: Cricut Die-Cut Pieces

Cartridge	Page #	Keypad #	Basic Key	Shift	Mode	Paper Type	Qty.	Size
Home Accents	Pamphlet	1	Flower1	No		Brown cardstock	1	6"
Home Accents	Pamphlet	32	Border2	No	Auto fill	Brown cardstock	1	2"
Winter Woodland	57	26	Sqrrl-s	Yes		Brown cardstock	3	2"

Part 2: Assembly

1. Adhere the 6" flower die cut to the center front of the lampshade with an adhesive that will stick to the fabric on the lampshade.

2. Adhere the border die cuts along the bottom edge of lampshade.

Note: Overlap the borders slightly to create a seamless look.

3. After all the glue has dried, spray clear glaze to protect die-cut shapes on the shade.

Note: The clear glaze will allow you to dust or wipe the lampshade as needed for cleaning.

4. Attach hanging jewel decorations to the base corners of the lampshade.

Mon Amour

By Gabriela Villaseñor
Cricut Cuts: Intermediate Level

MATERIALS

- Love Struck Seasonal Cartridge (2010)
- Black photo or ATC tray with 2½" x 3½" squares
- Heart metal charm
- Key metal charm
- Adhesive
- Embellishment stickers
- Dimensional adhesive
- Ribbon: red and pink
- Flower embellishment
- Coarse glitter
- Glitter glue
- White paint dauber
- Glossy accents
- Border punch
- Adhesive pearls
- Pink cardstock
- Red cardstock
- Red and pink patterned paper (various patterns)
- ¾"-width ribbon
- Sewing machine

INSTRUCTIONS

Part 1: Cricut Die-Cut Pieces

Before cutting any pieces, change the settings to Units = ¹/10. For more information, see page 38.

Cartridge	Page #	Keypad #	Basic Key	Shift	Paper Type	Qty.	Size
Block 1:							
Love Struck	Pamphlet	39	Kiss	No	Red and pink cardstock (1 of each color)	2	1.3"
Block 2:							
Love Struck	Pamphlet	19	Heart9	No	Pink cardstock	1	2.40"
Block 4:							
Love Struck	Pamphlet	3	Heart3	No	Pink cardstock	1	2.50"
Middle Block 5:							
Love Struck	Pamphlet	2	Heart2	No	Red cardstock	1	2.40"
Block 7:							
Love Struck	Pamphlet	42	Love	No	Red cardstock	1	1.3"
Block 8:							
Love Struck	Pamphlet	29	Lips	No	Red cardstock	1	1.90"
Bottom Block 10:							
Love Struck	Pamphlet	43	Flirt	No	Red cardstock	1	2.1"
Block 11:							
Love Struck	Pamphlet	4	Heart4	No	Pink cardstock	1	2.8"

Part 2: Assembly

1. Cut 12 pieces of patterned paper to 2½" x 3½" size for background pieces.

2. Distress all patterned paper pieces.

3. Decide which pieces will go in each box.

Top Row of Blocks: Block 1

1. Add glossy accents to the red "kiss" die cut.

2. Sprinkle glitter on the heart above the "i" on the red "kiss" die cut.

3. Sew 1/2" strip of paper onto background pattern in a diagonal position.

4. Adhere paper from step 6 to block 1.

5. Adhere pink "kiss" die cut to center of block 1.

6. When dry, adhere red "kiss" die cut from step 4 on top of pink piece to show pink piece as a shadow.

Block 2

1. Adhere patterned paper to block 2.

2. Adhere pink heart die cut to the center of the patterned paper.

3. Use glitter glue to highlight some of the heart shapes.

Block 3

1. Wrap 3/4"-width ribbon around the left side of the patterned paper and adhere to block 3.

2. Adhere a paper embellishment sticker or love sentiment to block 3 using dimensional tape.

Block 4

1. Adhere patterned paper to block 4.

2. Adhere heart3 die cut to center of the patterned paper for block 4.

3. Use red glitter glue to cover the small heart shape and kissing couple.

Middle Row of Blocks: Block 5

1. Adhere patterned paper to block 5.

2. Apply glossy accents on the outer edge of the heart2 die cut.

3. Apply glitter around the edges of the die cut.

4. Adhere heart2 die cut to the center of the patterned paper for block 5.

5. Apply glitter to the middle of die cut.

Block 6

1. Adhere patterned paper to block 6.

2. Adhere a flower embellishment to the center of the patterned paper for block 6.

3. Adhere pearls to left side of block 6.

Block 7

1. Adhere patterned paper to block 7.

2. Use a border punch on red cardstock to create a trim piece.

3. Adhere border from step 2 to bottom of block 7.

4. Adhere "love" die cut at an angle in the center of the patterned paper for block 7.

5. Adhere glossy accents on the small heart.

6. Adhere glitter on the swirl part of die cut.

Block 8

1. Adhere patterned paper to block 8.

2. Adhere lips die cut to center of patterned paper for block 8.

3. Apply glossy accents on the lips die cut.

Bottom Row of Blocks: Block 9

1. Tie a bow with pink ribbon, and wrap the ends of the ribbon around a red piece of patterned paper.

2. Adhere paper from step 1 to the patterned paper for block 9.

3. Adhere a love sentiment or paper embellishment sticker to the corner of block 9.

Block 10

1. Adhere patterned paper to block 10.

2. Adhere "flirt" die cut at an angle to the center of the patterned paper for block 10.

3. Adhere glossy accents on the small heart.

4. Adhere glitter on the swirl part of die cut.

Block 11

1. Add white paint to the edges of heart4 die cut.

2. Sew heart4 die cut to the center of the patterned paper for block 11.

3. Adhere piece from step 2 to block 11.

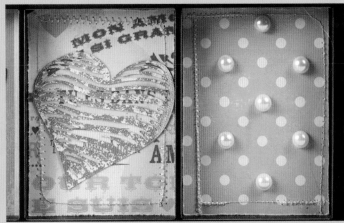

Block 12

1. Sew border around patterned paper.

2. Adhere patterned paper to block 12.3. Adhere pearls as desired to block 12.

Finishing touches

Add coordinating ribbons to the hanger on the top of the tray.

Carte Postale

By Cathie Rigby
Cricut Cuts: Intermediate Level

MATERIALS

- Sentimentals Cartridge
- French Manor Cartridge
- Stone Script Cartridge
- 6-drawer papier-mâché box
- Black paint
- Black ink
- Black-and-white damask patterned paper
- High-gloss black cardstock
- Cardstock (red, white, pink, light brown, blue, black)
- Red vinyl
- Transfer tape
- Adhesive
- Cricut tool kit

INSTRUCTIONS

Part 1: Cricut Die-Cut Pieces

Cartridge	Page #	Keypad #	Basic Key	Creative Feature Key	Shift	Mode	Function	Paper Type	Qty.	Size
Sentimentals	56	33	Quill		No		Flip	Black cardstock	1	2½"
Sentimentals	56	33	Quill-s		Yes		Flip	Light brown cardstock	1	2½"
Sentimentals	56	33	Quill	Layer	No		Flip	Blue cardstock	1	2½"
Sentimentals	55	32	Inkwell		No			Light brown cardstock	1	3¼"
Sentimentals	55	32	Inkwell	Layer	No			Black high-gloss cardstock	1	3¼"
French Manor	70	43	Stamp		No			Pink cardstock	1	1½"
French Manor	70	43	Stamp		No			White cardstock	1	1½"
French Manor	70	43	Stamp	Layer	No			Red cardstock	1	1½"
Stone Script	Pamphlet		S, t, a, m, p, s*		Yes on S	Fit to length		Red vinyl	1	5½"
Stone Script	Pamphlet		B, i, r, t, h, d, a, y, s*		Yes on B	Fit to length		Red vinyl	1	5½"
Stone Script	Pamphlet		W, e, d, d, i, n, g, s*		Yes on W	Fit to length		Red vinyl	1	5½"
Stone Script	Pamphlet		B, a, b, y*		Yes on B	Fit to length		Red vinyl	1	5½"
Stone Script	Pamphlet		S, y, m, p, a, t, h, y		Yes on S	Fit to length		Red vinyl	1	5½"
Stone Script	Pamphlet		T, h, a, n, k, Y, o, u		Yes on T and Y	Fit to length		Red vinyl	1	5½"

Note: You may label drawers as you wish. These are just some examples.

Part 2: Assembly

1 Paint top, back, and front of box with black acrylic paint.

Note: Do not apply too many coats since this will cause the paper to bubble.

2. Cut 2 damask patterned paper pieces measuring 6½" x 12" each and ink all corners.

3. Adhere paper to sides of box with decoupage applied to the paper and the box.

4. Smooth paper with the scraper tool to remove any bubbles.

5. Cut black cardstock to 6⅛" x 6½".

6. Fold black cardstock in half and score ½" from each side to form an easel.

7. Ink the edges of the brown and blue die-cut pieces.

8. Assemble die-cut pieces, as shown, and adhere to the front of the easel. Attach easel to top of box with adhesive.

9. Use transfer tape to pick up and place vinyl letters on the center of the drawers.

Note: For tips using vinyl, see page 28.

10. Apply paint or paper to the inside of drawers, as desired.

Note: Allow paint to dry thoroughly before placing greeting cards inside the drawers.

Memories

By Cathie Rigby
Cricut Cuts: Intermediate Level

MATERIALS

- Accent Essentials Cartridge
- Home Décor Cartridge
- Storybook Cartridge
- Art Philosophy Cartridge
- Indie Art Solutions Cartridge
- Home Accents Cartridge
- Tie the Knot Cartridge
- From My Kitchen Cartridge
- Sentimentals Cartridge
- Plantin Schoolbook Cartridge
- Dimensional adhesive
- Lush shaped album by Making Memories
- Ribbon: red, black, sheer and grosgrain
- Large silk leaf
- Large flower embellishment in red and white
- Small paper flowers
- Flourish punch or die cut
- White glitter paint spray
- Gems
- Brads
- Heart and key embellishment charms
- Embellishment charm
- Swivel clasp
- White glitter glue
- Velvet textured patterned paper
- Mulberry paper
- Black craft foam
- Letter stamps
- Glossy accents
- Border punch
- Adhesive pearls
- Cardstock
- Gel pen
- Black pen
- Red inkpad
- Black inkpad

INSTRUCTIONS

Part 1: Cricut Die-Cut Pieces for Cover

Cartridge	Page #	Keypad #	Basic Key	Creative Feature Key	Shift	Paper Type	Qty.	Size
Storybook	45		Tulip1		Yes	Red cardstock	2 of each size	3", 2½", 2"
Storybook	33		Cockatoo		Yes	Red cardstock	1	1½"
Accent Essentials	37	6	Accnt6s	Shadow	Yes	White cardstock	6	2¼"
Home Décor	Pamphlet	41	Memories		Yes	Black cardstock	1	1½"

Part 2: Assembly

1. Fussy cut velvet damask pattern from patterned paper and adhere to left edge of the cover.

2. Adhere 3 tulip die cuts left to right, from large to small, ending in the lower-right corner.

3. Remove the tulip heads from 3 more tulip die cuts, and use the swirls to fill in the space to the bottom and right of album.

4. Spray white glitter paint on 6 scallop die cuts, and wrinkle each one.

5. Gently open wrinkled scallops and stack to form flower.

6. Place jeweled brad in the center of the flower and shape petals before the paint completely dries.

7. Layer the cream flower over the black paper flower and large red flower embellishment.

8. Adhere the flower stack to the lower-left corner of the album cover.

9. Adhere silk leaf behind flower.

10. Adhere "Memories" die cut to album.

11. Adhere small flowers to the upper-right corner of the album cover.

12. Attach small gems to the center of flowers from step 11.

13. Ink the edges of album with red ink, as desired.

Part 3: Cricut Die-Cut Pieces for Pages 1 and 2

Cartridge	Page #	Keypad #	Basic Key	Creative Feature Key	Shift	Paper Type	Qty.	Size
Indie Art	Pamphlet	4	Buterfly		No	White cardstock	1	2.2"
Art Philosophy	66	46	Flower2	Layer	Yes	Red cardstock	1	2.7"
From My Kitchen	45	18	Cutbrd	Tab	No	Red cardstock	1	2¼"
Home Accents	Pamphlet	21	Corner1		No	Black cardstock	1	2"
Tie the Knot	25	2	Flrsh1-s		Yes	Black cardstock	1	1½"
Tie the Knot	25	2	Flrsh1-s	Blackout/Shadow	Yes	White cardstock	1	1½"

Part 4: Assembly

1. Cut red patterned paper to cover page 1 and red cardstock to cover page 2.

2. Adhere background papers to album.

3. Cut a 3½" x 7½" strip of white patterned paper, tear right edge ½", and ink the edges.

4. Adhere strip to the left side of page 1.

5. Cut a 4¼" x 6¼" photo mat out of pre-embossed black cardstock, and punch a half-circle out of the top.

6. Adhere the photo mat to page 1, leaving the top open, so the mat can also be a pocket.

7. Cut a small corner from the damask patterned paper and adhere to the upper-right corner of the pocket.

8. Cut a 4⅞" x 4¼" piece of damask patterned paper.

9. Adhere the damask patterned paper on a red piece of cardstock measuring 5" x 4½".

10. Adhere the tab die-cut piece to the left side and write "dream" with white gel pen.

Note: This can be used for another photo or for journaling.

11. Put the tabbed card in the pocket.

12. Adhere red round flourish to the lower left of page 1.

13. Adhere a black flower with gem brad on top of the flourish from step 10.

14. Adhere the black flourish to lower-right corner of page 1.

15. Adhere butterfly over the black flourish.

16. Add glitter glue to the butterfly and gems to the antennas.

17. Cut 2 photo mats measuring 3" x 4" each.

18. Punch 2 photo corners and add to mats.

19. Cut 2¼" x 6½" strip of white patterned paper.

20. Adhere paper strip from step 18 to bottom of page 2.

21. Adhere photo mats to page 2.

22. Layer black flourish die cut on white shadow piece.

23. Adhere layered die cut to upper-right corner.

24. Create a 2" journaling circle, and attach a red ribbon to the circle with brad.

25. Adhere journaling circle to page 2.

Part 5: Cricut Die-Cut Pieces for Pages 3 and 4

Cartridge	Page #	Keypad #	Basic Key	Creative Feature Key	Shift	Paper Type	Qty.	Size
Home Décor	Pamphlet	49	Adore		No	Red dot patterned paper	1	1½"
Home Décor	Pamphlet	49	Adore	Shadow	No	Red cardstock	1	1½"

Part 6: Assembly

1. Cut black flower patterned paper to cover page 3 and red and white strip patterned paper to cover page 4.

2. Adhere background papers to pages 3 and 4.

3. Cut a 7¾" x 4" piece of black flower patterned paper and adhere to center of page 4.

4. Adhere black mulberry paper to the upper and lower edges of the piece from step 3.

5. Cut a 5½" x 5½" piece of red dot patterned paper.

6. Cut a 5⅝" x 5⅝" piece of white cardstock and adhere to the back of the piece from step 6.

7. Attach brads to each corner and adhere layered photo mat to the center of page 3.

8. Tie a bow with red ribbon and attach to top of the photo mat from step 7.

9. Stamp a sentiment onto a small piece of white cardstock, and attach small red heart brad.

10. Layer sentiment on piece of red cardstock and black mulberry paper.

11. Adhere sentiment piece over photo mat on page 3.

12. Adhere 2 black punched flourishes to the lower-right side of page 4.

13. Adhere large red and black flower embellishment with large gem in the center to page 4.

14. Adhere "Adore" die cut to upper-right side of page 4.

15. Adhere 3 small gems to the upper left of page 4.

Part 7: Cricut Die-Cut Pieces for Pages 5 and 6

Cartridge	Page #	Keypad #	Basic Key	Shift	Paper Type	Qty.	Size
Tie the Knot	25	2	Flrsh1-s	Yes	Black cardstock	1	1¼"
Tie the Knot	54	31	Love	No	Black vinyl	1	1"
Tie the Knot	37	14	Heart2-s	Yes	Red vinyl	1	1"
Storybook	45	14	Tulip1	Yes	Red velvet paper	1	3"

Part 8: Assembly

1. Cut black cardstock to cover page 5 and red damask patterned paper to cover page 6.

2. Adhere background papers to pages.

3. Cut 1½" x 8" strip of white and red striped patterned paper.

4. Tear and ink strip and tie red ribbon to right side.

5. Adhere piece to bottom of page 5.

6. Cut a 3½" x 5¼" photo mat from red damask patterned paper and adhere to page 5.

7. Cut a 2½" x 4" journaling square from white cardstock.

8. Punch small tag shape from red cardstock and fold over top of square to create tab.

9. Adhere journaling block to page 5.

10. Use a white gel pen to write "Cherish" on the bottom of page 5.

11. Add black flourish die cut to bottom of photo mat on page 5.

12. Cut a 2¾" x 7" piece of striped paper and adhere to page 6, as shown.

13. Cut a 4½" x 6" photo mat from black patterned paper and round corners with a punch.

14. Adhere a black ribbon to the bottom of photo mat on page 6.

15. Adhere 2 red jewels to ends of the ribbon from step 14.

16. Adhere completed photo page to page 6.

17. Add red velvet flourish to the upper left of page 6 with dimensional adhesive.

18. Attach black name plate to page 6 above photo mat.

19. Punch a 1⅛" x 1¾" tag shape to slide in name plate.

20. Adhere vinyl die cut and heart piece to tag.

21. Attach ribbon to tag, and insert tag in name plate.

22. Cut small piece of black cardstock and write "You" with a white gel pen.

23. Insert black cardstock from step 22 in the name plate.

Part 9: Cricut Die-Cut Pieces for Pages 7 and 8

Cartridge	Page #	Keypad #	Basic Key	Creative Feature Key	Shift	Paper Type	Qty.	Size
Sentimentals	36	13	Key1			Red cardstock	1	2½"
Sentimentals	36	13	Key1	Shadow		Black cardstock	1	2½"
Home Accents	Pamphlet	21	Corner1		No	Black cardstock	1	2"
Home Décor	Pamphlet	47	Forever		No	White cardstock	1	1½"

Part 10: Assembly

1. Cut 2 black patterned papers for pages 7 and 8.

2. Adhere background papers to pages 7 and 8.

3. Cut a 6½" x 5½" square of striped patterned paper and adhere to the center of page 7.

4. Cut a 3½" x 4¼" photo mat from red cardstock.

5. Cut a 3" x 4" photo mat from black cardstock.

6. Distress the edges of the black photo mat.

7. Attach a heart clip to a black ribbon and attach black ribbon to the top of the red photo mat.

8. Adhere the red photo mat to page 7.

9. Tie a knot in a red ribbon and attach to the bottom of the black photo mat.

10. Add a brad at each end of the red ribbon.

11. Adhere the black photo mat to page 7.

12. Layer red key die cut on black shadow die cut.

13. Attach a black grommet to the assembled key die cut.

14. Add key details with a white gel pen, attach small black eyelet, as shown, and attach to page 7.

15. Stack black, white, and red flowers and attach a keyhole embellishment to the center.

16. Adhere assembled flower to the bottom of page 7.

17. Wrap black satin ribbon across entire page 8 and adhere to back.

18. Tie bow with separate black ribbon and attach to page 8.

19. Cut a 3½" x 4¾" piece of white patterned paper.

20. Cut a 2¾" x 4" piece of red dot patterned paper and adhere to white patterned paper from step 19.

21. Adhere photo mat from step 20 to page 8.

22. Adhere black flourish die cut to the lower corner of the photo mat on page 8.

23. Cut a 2½" x 3½" piece of red cardstock and adhere to page 8.

24. Cut a 1¾" x 3¼" piece of white patterned paper, and layer on top red cardstock piece from step 23.

25. Ink "Forever" die cut with black ink.

26. Adhere "Forever" die cut to page 8.

27. Add white glitter glue over "Forever" letters.

Part 11: Cricut Die-Cut Pieces for Pages 9 and 10

Cartridge	Page #	Keypad #	Basic Key	Shift	Paper Type	Qty.	Size
Accent Essentials	79	48	Accnt48	Yes	Black craft foam*	1	3"
Accent Essentials	79	48	Accnt48	Yes	White craft foam*	1	3"
Storybook	33		Cockatoo	Yes	Red cardstock	1	2½"
Plantin Schoolbook	68		Brace	No	White striped patterned paper	1	3"
Plantin Schoolbook	68		Brace	No	Chipboard*	1	3"

*Use a deep-cut blade, if available.

Part 12: Assembly

1. Cut red dot patterned papers to cover pages 9 and 10.

2. Adhere background papers to album.

3. Attach sentiment sticker to the top of page 9.

4. Cut a 3½" x 5¾" piece of black cardstock.

5. Tie a knot in a piece of 6" red and white sheer ribbon.

6. Create a pocket by wrapping sheer ribbon around the black cardstock from step 4.

7. Adhere assembled ribbon and cardstock to page 9.

8. Cut a 3¾" x 2¾" piece of red damask patterned paper and adhere to the white foam die cut.

9. Cut a 3¾" x 2¾" piece of black damask patterned paper and adhere to the black foam die cut.

10. Attach red jewels around black foam frame.

11. Attach black jewels around the white foam frame.

12. Tuck the foam frames under the ribbon on page 9.

13. Punch a black piece of cardstock with a 2½" scalloped circle punch.

14. Cut a 7¾" x 4½" piece of black damask patterned paper and adhere to page 10.

15. Adhere black velvet rickrack to the top and bottom of the paper from step 14, as shown.

16. Cut a 4½" x 3¾" piece of red cardstock and adhere to page 10.

17. Add embellishment around red cardstock with black pen.

18. Adhere bracket die-cut paper onto chipboard bracket die cuts.

19. Adhere assembled bracket die cuts to the sides of the red cardstock from step 17.

20. Adhere red jewels around the edges of the scallop circle from step 13.

21. Adhere cockatoo to scallop circle and add marker and ink details.

Seasonal Charm

By Susan McNees
Cricut Cuts: Intermediate Level

MATERIALS FOR SPRING

- Simply Charmed Cartridge
- Ashlyn's Alphabet Cartridge
- Cotton fabric (dark brown, light blue, dark blue, yellow, 3 different pink patterns, light green, dark green, green dot, white with green accents, red)
- Heavy-duty fusible webbing
- Sewing machine
- Thread
- Quilt batting

INSTRUCTIONS FOR SPRING

Part 1: Fabric Preparation

1. Cut 7" x 7" pieces of fabric from the dark brown and light blue fabrics.

2. Cut 4" x 4" pieces of the dark blue, light green, and yellow fabrics.

3. Cut a 3" x 3" piece of yellow fabric.

4. Cut a 4" x 3" piece of first pink fabric.

5. Cut a 14" x 10" piece of dark green fabric.

6. Cut 6" x 6" pieces from second and third patterned pink fabrics and red fabric.

7. Cut a 4" x 12" piece of green dot fabric.

8. Cut heavy-duty fusible webbing for each piece of fabric cut.

9. Iron the fusible webbing to the back of each fabric piece, according to webbing instructions.

10. When the fabric is cool, remove the paper backing from fabric piece before placing on Cricut the mat.

11. Cut two 16½" x 17" pieces of the white-with-green-accents fabric.

12. Cut three 2" x 5½" pieces of the white-with-green-accents fabric.

13. Cut one 16¼" x 16¾" piece of quilt batting.

Part 2: Cricut Die-Cut Pieces

Cartridge	Page #	Keypad #	Basic Key	Shift	Creative Feature Key	Paper Type	Qty.	Size
Simply Charmed	36	9	BirdFly	Yes		7" x 7" dark brown fabric	1	5"
Simply Charmed	36	9	BirdFly	Yes	Layer1	7" x 7" light blue fabric	1	5"
Simply Charmed	36	9	BirdFly	Yes	Layer2	4" x 4" dark blue fabric	1	5"
Simply Charmed	36	9	BirdFly	Yes	Layer3	3" x 3" yellow fabric	1	5"
Simply Charmed	36	9	BirdFly	Yes	Layer4	4" x 3" first pink fabric	1	5"
Simply Charmed	38	11	Flower1	No		14" x 10" dark green fabric	2	8¾"
Simply Charmed	38	11	Flower1	No	Layer1	6" x 6" second pink patterned fabric	1	8¾"
Simply Charmed	38	11	Flower1	No	Layer1	6" x 6" third pink patterned fabric	1	8¾"

Part 2: Cricut Die-Cut Pieces (Continued)

Cartridge	Page #	Keypad #	Basic Key	Shift	Creative Feature Key	Paper Type	Qty.	Size
Simply Charmed	38	11	Flower1	No	Layer4	6" x 6" red fabric	2	8¾"
Simply Charmed	38	11	Flower1	No	Layer3	4" x 4" yellow fabric	2 (for Stamen only)	8¾"
Simply Charmed	38	11*	Flower1	No	Layer3	4" x 4" light green fabric	2 (Press Stop after leaf strip)	8¾"
Ashlyn's Alphabet	46, 43, 45, 36, 41, 34		S, p, r, i, n, g	Yes on S		4" x 12" green dot fabric	1 of each letter	3"

*Note: Use the Repeat Last button to make this cut easier.

Part 3: Assembly

1. Reduce fabric bulk on die-cut pieces by trimming away fabric that will not be seen.

Note: This will make it easier to sew through all layers.

2. Iron on "spring" letters to the top of one 16½" x 17" piece of the white-with-green-accents background fabric, as shown.

3. Assemble the bird and flower die-cut pieces on the background fabric as you want them to appear.

4. Iron on the bird and flower die-cut pieces.

5. Appliqué around the die-cut images.

6. Layer second background fabric piece on top of the front piece, with right sides facing.

7. Layer batting on top of fabric and sew a ¼" seam around all edges except the top.

8. Turn fabric right side out.

9. Fold the three 2" x 5½" strips in half so each strip is 2" x 2¾".

10. Sew a ¼" seam on long cut edge.

11. Turn fabric right side out and fold in half.

12. Insert strips between layers of main project layers and sew top closed.

13. Sew seam ¼" from the edge around all 4 sides of the project.

14. Use a curtain rod or dowel and ribbon to hang on the wall.

MATERIALS FOR SUMMER

- Simply Charmed Cartridge
- Birthday Bash Cartridge
- Cotton fabric (red, blue, and light brown striped; orange; light brown; yellow; light blue)
- Heavy-duty fusible webbing
- Sewing machine
- Thread
- Quilt batting

INSTRUCTIONS FOR SUMMER

Part 1: Fabric Preparation

1. Cut 12" x 12" pieces from the striped and light brown fabrics.

2. Cut an 8" x 8" piece from the orange fabric.

3. Cut a 6" x 4" piece from the yellow fabric.

4. Cut a 5" x 12" piece from the striped fabric.

5. Cut heavy-duty fusible webbing for each piece of fabric cut.

6. Iron the fusible webbing to the back of each fabric piece, according to webbing instructions.

7. When the fabric is cool, remove the paper backing from fabric piece before placing on Cricut mat.

8. Cut two 16½" x 17" pieces of the white-with-blue-accents fabric.

9. Cut three 2" x 5½" pieces of the white-with-blue-accents fabric.

10. Cut one 16¼" x 16¾" piece of quilt batting.

Part 2: Cricut Die-Cut Pieces

Cartridge	Page #	Keypad #	Basic Key	Shift	Creative Feature Key	Function	Paper Type	Qty.	Size
Simply Charmed	51	24	Sand	No			12" x 12" striped fabric	1	10¼"
Simply Charmed	51	24	Sand	No	Layer2		8" x 8" orange fabric	1	10¼"
Simply Charmed	51	24	Sand	No	Layer3	Mat Size 24"	12" x 12" light brown fabric	1	10¼"
Simply Charmed	51	24	Sand	No	Layer4		6" x 4" yellow fabric	1 (Press **Stop** after triangle piece)	10¼"
Birthday Bash	42, 37, 57, 57, 33, 34	22, 17, 37, 37, 13, 14*	S, u, m, m, e, r	Yes on S	Font		5" x 12" striped fabric	1	2"

*Tip: When using a font found inside of a shape cartridge, use the keypad from a font cartridge, like Plantin Schoolbook, to make finding the letters easier.

Part 3: Assembly

1. Reduce fabric bulk on die-cut pieces by trimming away fabric that will not be seen.

Note: This will make it easier to sew through all layers.

2. Cut a piece of blue fabric for the back of the "summer" letters.

3. Iron the fusible webbing to the back of the blue fabric piece, according to webbing instructions.

4. Iron on "summer" letters to the blue fabric.

5. Iron on fabric piece from step 4 to the top of one $16\frac{1}{2}$" x 17" piece of the white-with-blue-accents background fabric.

6. Assemble the sand, pail, and shovel die-cut pieces on the background fabric.

7. Iron on the sand, pail, and shovel die-cut pieces to the background fabric.

8. Appliqué around the die-cut images.

9. Layer second background fabric piece on top of the front piece, with right sides facing.

10. Layer batting on top of fabric and sew a $\frac{1}{4}$" seam around all edges except the top.

11. Turn fabric right side out.

12. Fold the three 2" x $5\frac{1}{2}$" strips in half so each strip is 2" x $2\frac{3}{4}$".

13. Sew a $\frac{1}{4}$" seam on long cut edge.

14. Turn fabric right side out and fold in half.

15. Insert strips between layers of main project layers and sew top closed.

16. Sew seam $\frac{1}{4}$" from the edge around all 4 sides of the project.

17. Use a curtain rod or dowel and ribbon to hang on the wall.

- Simply Charmed Cartridge
- Batman® Cartridge
- Cotton fabric (light green, orange, yellow, light brown, dark brown)
- Heavy-duty fusible webbing
- Sewing machine
- Thread
- Quilt batting

Part 1: Fabric Preparation

1. Cut 10" x 10" and 4" x 8" pieces of the light green, orange, and yellow fabrics.

2. Cut a 12" x 12" piece of dark brown fabric.

3. Cut a 5" x 12" piece of the orange fabric.

4. Cut heavy-duty fusible webbing for each piece of fabric cut.

5. Iron the fusible webbing to the back of each fabric piece, according to webbing instructions.

6. When the fabric is cool, remove the paper backing from fabric piece before placing on Cricut mat.

7. Cut two 16½" x 17" pieces of the light brown fabric.

8. Cut three 2" x 5½" pieces of the light brown fabric.

9. Cut one 16¼" x 16¾" piece of quilt batting.

Part 2: Cricut Die-Cut Pieces

Cartridge	Page #	Keypad #	Basic Key	Shift	Creative Feature Key	Paper Type	Qty.	Size
Simply Charmed	55	28	Tree3	Yes		10" x 10" light green fabric	1	7½"
Simply Charmed	55	28	Tree3	Yes		10" x 10" orange fabric	1	7½"
Simply Charmed	55	28	Tree3	Yes		10" x 10" yellow fabric	1	7½"
Simply Charmed	55	28	Tree3	Yes	Layer4	4" x 8" light green fabric	1	7½"
Simply Charmed	55	28	Tree3	Yes	Layer4	4" x 8" orange fabric	1	7½"
Simply Charmed	55	28	Tree3	Yes	Layer4	4" x 8" yellow fabric	1	7½"
Simply Charmed	55	28	Tree3	No	Layer1	12" x 12" dark brown fabric	3	7½"
Batman®	55	28	"Fall"	Yes	Font	5" x 12" orange fabric	1	2½"

BATMAN: THE BRAVE AND THE BOLD and all related characters and elements are trademarks of and © DC Comics. CARTOON NETWORK and logo are trademarks of and © Cartoon Network. WBSHIELD: TM & © Warner Bros. Entertainment, Inc.

Part 3: Assembly

1. Reduce fabric bulk on die-cut pieces by trimming away fabric that will not be seen.

Note: This will make it easier to sew through all layers.

2. Iron on "fall" letters to the top of one 16½" x 17" piece of the light brown background fabric, as shown.

3. Assemble the tree die-cut pieces on the background fabric as you want them to appear.

4. Iron on the tree die-cut pieces.

5. Appliqué around the die-cut images.

6. Layer second background fabric piece on top of the front piece, with right sides facing.

7. Layer batting on top of fabric and sew a ¼" seam around all edges except the top.

8. Turn fabric right side out.

9. Fold the three 2" x 5½" strips in half so each strip is 2" x 2¾".

10. Sew a ¼" seam on long cut edge.

11. Turn fabric right side out and fold in half.

12. Insert strips between layers of main project layers and sew top closed.

13. Sew seam ¼" from the edge around all 4 sides of the project.

14. Use a curtain rod or dowel and ribbon to hang on the wall.

MATERIALS FOR WINTER

- Simply Charmed Cartridge
- Superman® Cartridge
- Cotton fabric (aqua dot, aqua striped, light yellow snowflake, blue snowflake, light blue)
- Heavy-duty fusible webbing
- Sewing machine
- Thread
- Quilt batting

INSTRUCTIONS FOR WINTER

Part 1: Fabric Preparation

1. Cut two 7½" x 10" and two 9" x 10" pieces of the aqua dot fabric.

2. Cut a 4" x 10" piece of the aqua striped fabric.

3. Cut 4" x 12" pieces of the light yellow snowflake and blue snowflake fabrics.

4. Cut heavy-duty fusible webbing for each piece of fabric cut.

5. Iron the fusible webbing to the back of each fabric piece, according to webbing instructions.

6. When the fabric is cool, remove the paper backing from fabric piece before placing on Cricut the mat.

7. Cut two 16½" x 17" pieces of the light blue fabric.

8. Cut three 2" x 5½" pieces of the light blue fabric.

9. Cut one 16¼" x 16¾" piece of quilt batting.

Part 2: Cricut Die-Cut Pieces

Cartridge	Page #	Keypad #	Basic Key	Shift	Creative Feature Key	Mode	Function	Paper Type	Qty.	Size
Simply Charmed	65	38	Mitten	No		Mix 'n Match		7½" x 10" aqua dot fabric	1	5¾"
Simply Charmed	65	38	Mitten	No		Mix 'n Match	Flip	7½" x 10" aqua dot fabric	1	5¾"
Simply Charmed	65	38	Mitten	No	Layer2	Mix 'n Match		4" x 10" aqua striped fabric	1	5¾"
Simply Charmed	65	38	Mitten	No	Layer2	Mix 'n Match	Flip	4" x 10" aqua striped fabric	1	5¾"
Simply Charmed	65	38	Hat	Yes				9" x 10" aqua dot fabric	1	6½"
Superman®	39, 45, 63, 42, 40, 14	12, 18, 36, 15, 13, 14	W, i, n, t, e, r	Yes on W	Font			4" x 12" light yellow snowflake fabric		3"
Superman®	39, 45, 63, 42, 40, 14	12, 18, 36, 15, 13, 14	W, i, n, t, e, r	Yes on W	Font Shadow			4" x 12" blue snowflake fabric		3"

SUPERMAN and all related characters and elements are trademarks of and © DC Comics. WBSHIELD: TM & © Warner Bros. Entertainment, Inc. (s10)

Part 3: Assembly

1. Reduce fabric bulk on die-cut pieces by trimming away fabric that will not be seen.

Note: This will make it easier to sew through all layers.

2. Iron on "winter" letters to the shadow blue fabric letters.

3. Iron on assembled "winter" letters to the top of one 16½" x 17" piece of the light blue background fabric.

4. Assemble the mitten and hat die-cut pieces on the background fabric as desired.

5. Iron on the hat and mitten die-cut pieces.

6. Appliqué around the die-cut images.

7. Layer second background fabric piece on top of the front piece, with right sides facing.

8. Layer batting on top of fabric and sew a ¼" seam around all edges except the top.

9. Turn fabric right side out. Fold the three 2" x 5½" strips in half so each strip is 2" x 2¾".

10. Sew a ¼" seam on long cut edge.

11. Turn fabric right side out and fold in half.

12. Insert strips between layers of main project layers and sew top closed.

13. Sew seam ¼" from the edge around all 4 sides of the project.

14. Use a curtain rod or dowel and ribbon to hang on the wall.

Bless This Home

By June Houck
Cricut Cuts: Intermediate Level

MATERIALS

- Wall Décor and More Cartridge
- Light brown cardstock
- Dark brown cardstock
- White cardstock
- Red cardstock
- Blank sheet of paper (for template)
- Adhesive
- Gold pen
- Patterned paper (4 coordinating patterns)
- Olive metallic paper
- Frame
- Bone folder

INSTRUCTIONS

Part 1: Preparation

1. Cut 23 strips of patterned paper to 1" thickness each.

Note: The longest strip should be about 5", and strips should gradually get smaller in length.

2. Fold over one edge of each strip at $1/4$".

Note: Use a bone folder to make a good crease.

3. Place a 5" x 7" piece of light brown cardstock on mat horizontally.

4. Use navigation keys to place blade in the center in order to use Center Point function.

Part 2: Cricut Die-Cut Pieces

Cartridge	Page #	Keypad #	Basic Key	Shift	Creative Feature Key	Function	Paper Type	Qty.	Size
Wall Décor and More	37	10	Pear-s	Yes		Center Point	Light brown cardstock and white cardstock (for template)	2	$3^{3/4}$"
Wall Décor and More	70	43	Scissor	No	Font		Red cardstock	1	1"

Part 3: Iris Folding Pattern

1. Use the white cardstock pear shape to trace a pear on a blank sheet of paper.

2. Starting at the base of the pear, draw a straight line up and to the left. The section should not be higher than $1/4$" at its thickest point.

Note: Line lengths will vary.

3. Label this area "1."

4. Starting at the endpoint of area 1, draw another straight line up the left side of the pear $1/4$" thick at the thickest part.

5. Label this area "2."

6. From area 2 endpoint, draw another ¼" thick straight line to the right side of the pear.

7. Label this area "3."

8. Continue from each previous endpoint in a clockwise direction.

9. Area "4" is the lower-left side of the pear.

Note: You should now be at the original starting point of area "1."

10. The next start point will be ¼" before the area 1 start point (on the area 4 line segment) and will end ¼" before the area 1 endpoint. (This is area 5.)

11. Continue drawing lines in this manner until you have a small center, as shown.

Part 4: Iris Folding Instructions

1. Tape template on flat surface with removable tape.

2. With removable tape, tape the light brown cardstock die-cut piece on top of the template with the front facing down.

Note: Make sure the pear shape on the template lines up with die-cut pear on the cardstock.

3. Place the longest paper strip over area 1 so the folded side will show through to the front.

4. Add adhesive to the edges of the strip so it will stick to the cardstock and not the template.

5. Repeat steps 1-3 in a clockwise progression for areas 2-23, as shown, until the center is the only portion not covered.

Note: Make sure the strips are not glued around the stem and leaf of the pear since the edges of the strips will be trimmed so the patterned paper doesn't show through these areas.

6. Remove cardstock from the flat surface and turn over.

7. Trim the patterned paper around the outer edges of the cardstock so the patterned paper doesn't show through the pear stem or leaf.

Part 5: Assembly

1. Trim light brown cardstock to 4⅛" x 5⅝".

2. Adhere dark brown paper behind the leaf shape of the light brown cardstock.

3. Highlight the outer edges of the cardstock with a gold pen, as shown.

4. Cut a 4½" x 6" piece of olive metallic paper.

5. Adhere olive paper to the back of the project.

Note: The olive paper will show through the center of the iris-folded paper and through the pear stem.

6. Adhere red die-cut sentiment to the front of the finished piece.

7. Frame as desired in a 5" x 7" frame.

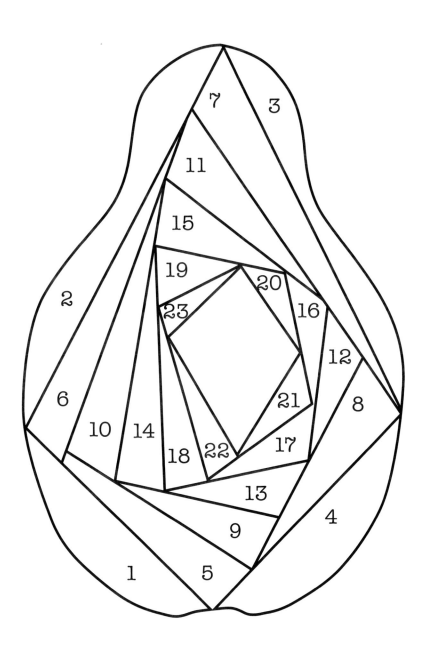

Warm Winter Wishes

By Cathie Rigby
Cricut Cuts: Intermediate Level

MATERIALS

- Winter Woodland Cartridge
- Mini Monsters Cartridge
- Wood sled
- Acrylic paint or wood stain
- Glue gun and glue sticks
- Decoupage medium, matte finish
- White, light blue, dark blue, light green, and dark brown cardstock
- Patterned paper

- Christmas items, such as pinecones, holly, or evergreen branches
- Silk flowers
- Foam paint brushes
- Chipboard, light or medium weight
- Jingle bells
- Glitter or dimensional snow
- Wire

INSTRUCTIONS

Part 1: Sled Preparation

1. Paint or stain wood sled using acrylic paint or wood stain.

Note: The sample project used 3 shades of acrylic paint: tan, silver, and burnt sienna. If you decide to paint the sled, you will need to use 2-3 coats, depending on the color.

2. Let the sled dry 15-20 minutes between coats.

Note: You do not need to cover the top of slats; they will be covered in paper.

Part 2: Cricut Die-Cut Pieces

Cartridge	Page #	Keypad #	Basic Key	Shift	Creative Feature Key	Mode	Paper Type	Qty.	Size
Winter Woodland	46	15	Snowman	No			White cardstock	1	7½"
Winter Woodland	46	15	Snwman-s	Yes			Light blue cardstock	1	7½"
Winter Woodland	46	15	Snwman-s	Yes	Layers		Dark blue cardstock	1	7½"
Winter Woodland	46	15	Snwman-s	Yes	Layers		Dark brown cardstock	1	7½"
Winter Woodland	46	15	Snwman-s	Yes	Shadow/Blackout	Multi Cut (3)	Chipboard*	1	7½"
Winter Woodland	67	36	WmWtrWsh	No	Shadow/Blackout		White cardstock	1	2½"
Winter Woodland	67	36	WmWtrWsh	No	Shadow/Blackout		Light blue cardstock	1	2½"
Mini Monsters	72	45	Fence2	Yes			Dark brown cardstock	1	3"
Mini Monsters	72	45	Fence2	Yes		Multi Cut (3)	Chipboard*	1	3"
Winter Woodland	37	6	Trees	No	Shadow/Blackout		Light green cardstock	1	8"
Winter Woodland	37	6	Trees	No	Shadow/Blackout	Multi Cut (3)	Chipboard*	1	8"

*Tip: Clean blade before cutting paper after cutting chipboard.

Part 3: Assembly

1. Glue cut images to chipboard.

2. Cut the trunk of one tree down so tree measures 6" tall.

3. Ink or distress the patterned paper as desired.

4. Cut patterned paper to the same size as the slats on the sled.

5. Glue patterned paper to slat with decoupage medium.

6. Glue shapes cut with the Cricut machine to the center of the sled.

7. Take 2-4 Christmas ornaments and arrange on sled as desired with hot glue.

8. Add silk flowers to the sled with hot glue.

Tip: Silk flowers can be used to cover holes or wire.

9. Glue the phrase where desired.

10. Add glitter or dimensional snow as desired.

11. Glue jingle bells to sled rope as desired with hot glue.

12. Add wire to hang on the door or wall.

Inspire Me

By Cathie Rigby
Cricut Cuts: Intermediate Level

MATERIALS

- Wall Décor and More Cartridge
- Home Accents Cartridge
- Large decorative wall mirror, 16" x 20"
- Cricut vinyl sheet, 12" x 24" (any color)
- Transfer tape
- Glass etching cream
- Popsicle stick

- Miscellaneous seashells
- Starfish
- Sea embellishments
- Florist moss
- Cricut tool kit
- Glue gun and sticks

INSTRUCTIONS

Part 1: Cricut Die-Cut Pieces

Note: Use a 12" x 24" mat for these cuts.

Cartridge	Page #	Keypad #	Basic Key	Shift	Mode	Paper Type	Qty.	Size
Wall Décor and More	38	11	Litehouse	No	Fit to Length and Portrait	Vinyl	1	15¾"*
Home Accents	Pamphlet	46	Inspire	No		Vinyl	1	2½"

*Note: The size can be adjusted based on the mirror size.

Part 2: Assembly

1. Remove vinyl from cutting mats.

2. Isolate image by cutting a 1" frame around each image.

Note: For tips on using vinyl with your Cricut, see page 28.

3. Using the hook tool from the Cricut tool kit, remove the inner images, leaving behind only a stencil.

Note: Leave behind the negative shapes. For example, on the lighthouse image, you will remove the actual lighthouse but leave the windows. On the phrase, you will remove the letters and leave the outlined shape.

4. Cut a piece of transfer tape for each die-cut piece.

Note: Make each piece of transfer tape large enough to cover the entire die-cut shape.

5. Remove red-lined backing paper and place the transfer tape over the top of each image.

6. Lightly rub transfer tape to flatten and straighten over image.

7. Flip over each die-cut piece and using the scraper from the tool kit, burnish the piece for a few seconds.

8. Carefully remove backing paper from the back of the each piece of vinyl.

Note: Make sure you wiggle the paper left to right to avoid tearing the vinyl.

9. Once paper has been completely removed, place the vinyl images right side up as desired on the mirror.

10. Tape off any areas of the mirror that will not be etched.

11. Using a Popsicle stick, place a generous amount of etching cream in all the openings.

Note: The etching cream should be the thickness of pancake batter over the open areas of the stencil.

12. Set timer for 10 minutes and allow the cream to set.

13. After 10 minutes, scrape the cream off the mirror and put the cream back in bottle.

14. Carefully rinse off the remainder of etching cream under lukewarm water.

Note: Wearing gloves is a good idea if you have sensitive skin. The cream contains acid.

15. Hot glue seashells in the lower-left corner of mirror.

16. Hot glue sea embellishments and starfish in the upper-right corner of mirror.

17. Hot glue floral moss to cover any holes left by sea shell placement.

Under the Big Top

By Cathie Rigby
Cricut Cuts: Advanced Level

MATERIALS

- Carousel Lite Cartridge
- Accent Essentials Cartridge
- Animal Kingdom Cartridge
- Plantin Schoolbook Cartridge
- Ikea-Luns chalk/magnetic board, 19" x 28"
- Inkpads colors: cocoa brown, light blue, and aqua
- Adhesive
- Heavy-duty ½" diameter magnets
- Hot-glue gun
- Glue sticks
- Crystal gems
- Vinyl (black, white)

- Transfer tape
- Dimensional adhesive
- Markers (red, black)
- Patterned paper (circus/animal-themed prints)
- Cardstock (blue, red, turquoise, orange, black, cream, light brown, white, yellow)
- Chipboard
- Small brads or half-backed jewels
- 2 red jewels
- 4 hitch fasteners
- Light turquoise acrylic paint
- ⅛" dowels

INSTRUCTIONS

Part 1: Chalkboard Preparation

1. Use light turquoise acrylic paint and paint the top frame portion of the chalkboard.

2. Let dry 5–7 minutes between coats.

Note: It should take 2 coats.

3. Cut 20 dowels to 6⁵⁄₁₆" pieces.

4. Glue dowels in place ½" apart to create animal cages out of the letter slots, as shown.

Note: Leave a larger opening in the center for small hands to reach in and pet the animals.

Part 2: Cricut Die-Cut Pieces

Cartridge	Page #	Keypad #	Basic Key	Shift	Mode	Function	Paper Type	Qty.	Size
Carousel	Pamphlet	45	Train3	No			Yellow cardstock	2	10"
Carousel	Pamphlet	45	Train3	No			Chipboard	2	10"
Accent Essentials	34	3	Accent3	No			Black vinyl	4	2½"
Carousel	Pamphlet	9	Tiger	No	Real Dial Size	Flip	Orange cardstock	1	4"
Carousel	Pamphlet	9	Tiger-s	No	Real Dial Size	Flip	Black cardstock	1	4"
Carousel	Pamphlet	5	Ticket	No			White cardstock	1	3¾"
Carousel	Pamphlet	5	Ticket-s	Yes			Turquoise cardstock	1	3¾"

Part 2: Cricut Die-Cut Pieces (Continued)

Cartridge	Page #	Keypad #	Basic Key	Creative Feature Key	Shift	Paper Type	Qty.	Size
Carousel	Pamphlet	11	RingMn-s		Yes	Chipboard	1	7½"
Carousel	Pamphlet	11	RingMn-s		Yes	White cardstock	1	7½"
Carousel	Pamphlet	11	RingMan		No	Black cardstock	1	7½"
Carousel	Pamphlet	11	RingMan		No	Red cardstock	1	7½"
Carousel	Pamphlet	14	Elephnt1-s		Yes	Pink cardstock	1	4"
Carousel	Pamphlet	14	Elephnt1-s		Yes	Chipboard	1	4"
Carousel	Pamphlet	14	Elephnt1		No	Gray cardstock	1	4"
Carousel	Pamphlet	3	Tent-s		Yes	Chipboard	1	5"
Carousel	Pamphlet	3	Tent-s		Yes	Blue cardstock	1	5"
Carousel	Pamphlet	3	Tent		No	Yellow cardstock	1	5"
Carousel	Pamphlet	12, 19, 22, 26	S, H, O, W	Font	No	Red cardstock	1	1"
Carousel	Pamphlet	12, 19, 22, 26	S-s, H-s, O-s, W-s	Font	Yes	White vinyl	1	1"
Carousel	Pamphlet	24	IcCrm1-s		Yes	Dark turquoise cardstock	1	3¼"
Carousel	Pamphlet	24	IcCrm1-s		Yes	Chipboard	1	3¼"
Carousel	Pamphlet	24	IceCream1		No	Light brown cardstock	1	3¼"
Carousel	Pamphlet	24	IceCream1		No	Pink cardstock	1	3¼"
Carousel	Pamphlet	50	Banner-s		Yes	Chipboard	1	2¼"
Carousel	Pamphlet	50	Banner-s		Yes	Red cardstock	1	2¼"
Carousel	Pamphlet	50	Banner		No	Yellow cardstock	1	2¼"
Animal Kingdom	112	31	Lion	Blackout	No	Chipboard	1	3"
Animal Kingdom	112	31	Lion		No	Mustard cardstock	1	3"
Animal Kingdom	112	31	Lion		No	Black cardstock	1	3"
Animal Kingdom	112	31	Lion-s		Yes	Light brown cardstock	1	3"
Animal Kingdom	112	31	Lion-s		Yes	Cream cardstock*	1	3"
Plantin Schoolbook	38, 49, 36, 32, 51, 50		G, r, e, a, t, e, s, t		Yes on G	White cardstock	1	.6"
Plantin Schoolbook	36, 45, 36, 32, 49, 51, 39		O, n, E, a, r, t, h		Yes on O and E	White cardstock	1	.6"
Plantin Schoolbook	54, 40, 43, 35, 32, 44, 50		W, i, l, d, A, n, i, m, a, l, s		Yes on W and A	Black vinyl	2	1"

*Note: You will use only the face portion of this cut.

Part 3: Assembly

1. Cut 2 strips of patterned paper measuring ½" wide and adhere to board underneath chalk trays.

2. Cut two 5½" x 8" pieces of chipboard to create a mini album that will be inserted into the right cage.

3. Cut four 5½" x 8" pieces of circus patterned paper and adhere to both sides of the chipboard.

4. Assemble ticket die cuts and add them to the cover of the chipboard mini album.

5. Assemble tiger die-cut pieces and adhere to the mini album cover.

6. Cut as many inside pages as desired out of white cardstock and insert in between chipboard pages.

7. Punch holes through the mini album in the upper-left corner and add a book ring to keep pages together.

8. Assemble tent die-cut pieces.

9. Add "Greatest on Earth" letters to the tent, as shown.

10. Use red and black markers to change the color of the flag and flagpole.

11. Add white vinyl to "SHOW" letters using transfer tape.

12. Attach "SHOW" letters to the center of tent with dimensional adhesive.

13. Add glitter glue to the letters.

14. Assemble the top and bottom of train die-cut pieces.

15. Attach the "wild animals" vinyl lettering to the top piece of each train.

16. Attach hitch fasteners to either side of the letters.

17. Adhere the top train pieces with hot glue to the top of letter opening.

18. Adhere the vinyl wheels to the bottom train die cuts.

19. Adhere red jewels to the center of the wheels with hot glue.

20. Adhere the bottom train die cuts to the bottom of letter openings.

Note: The bottom train die cuts will hang beyond the base of chalkboard.

21. Assemble elephant, lion, and banner die-cut pieces and glue 2 magnets to the back of each.

22. Insert the elephant into the cage on the left side.

23. Cut apart pink and brown die-cut pieces of ice cream apart and assemble.

24. Adhere 2 magnets to the back of the ice cream cone.

25. Assemble ring master and adhere 2 magnets to the back with hot glue.

26. Fussy cut ticket shapes from the patterned paper and adhere around the chalkboard frame.

27. Add a strip of Cricut magnet material to the left side of chalkboard.

Note: Magnets can be stored in the cages when the chalkboard is not in use.

Springtime Happiness

By Anita Wood
Cricut Cuts: Advanced Level

MATERIALS

- April Showers Cartridge
- Stamping Solutions Cartridge
- Plantin Schoolbook Cartridge
- Bloom Lite Cartridge
- Heritage Cartridge
- Home Accents Solutions Cartridge
- 12" x 12" white shadow box frame
- Inkpad colors: cocoa brown, light blue, and aqua
- Adhesive

- Dimensional adhesive
- Crystal gems
- Buttons
- Craft thread
- Patterned paper (blue, pink, yellow)
- Cardstock (green, pink, yellow, orange)
- Blue patterned cardstock
- Small brads or half-backed jewels
- Sewing machine
- Corner punch

INSTRUCTIONS

Part 1: Cricut Die-Cut Pieces

Cartridge	Page #	Keypad #	Basic Key	Shift	Paper Type	Qty.	Size
April Showers	Pamphlet	26	Banner	No	White cardstock	1	2"
April Showers	Pamphlet	36	BannrLyr	No	Blue, pink, and yellow cardstock	6 (2 of each color)	2"
April Showers	Pamphlet	5	Buttrfly	No	Wave blue patterned paper	2	1¼"
April Showers	Pamphlet	5	Buttrfly	No	Pink cardstock	2	1¼"
April Showers	Pamphlet	15	BtrfyLyr	No	Wave blue patterned paper	2	1¼"
April Showers	Pamphlet	15	BtrfyLyr	No	Flowered blue patterned paper	2	1¼"
April Showers	Pamphlet	5	Buttrfly	No	Pink or yellow cardstock	1	1½"
April Showers	Pamphlet	5	Buttrfly	No	Flowered blue patterned paper	1	1½"
April Showers	Pamphlet	15	BtrfyLyr	No	Wave blue patterned paper	1	1½"
April Showers	Pamphlet	15	BtrfyLyr	No	Pink or yellow cardstock	1	1½"
Stamping Solutions	Pamphlet	17	HpyBday*	No	Green patterned paper	1	2½"
Stamping Solutions	Pamphlet	17	HpyBday*	No	Blue cardstock	1	2½"
Bloom Lite	Pamphlet	20	Frame4	No	White cardstock	5	3"
Bloom Lite	Pamphlet	34	Flower9	No	Green, yellow, orange, or blue patterned paper	2	1¼"
Bloom Lite	Pamphlet	37	Flower12	No	Green, yellow, orange, or blue patterned paper	1	1¼"

*Note: You will only use the "happy" portion. Press Stop cut before the "birthday" portion cuts.

Part 1: Cricut Die-Cut Pieces (Continued)

Cartridge	Page #	Keypad #	Basic Key	Creative Feature Key	Shift	Paper Type	Qty.	Size
Bloom Lite	Pamphlet	40	Flower15	Layer	No	Green, yellow, orange, or blue patterned paper	1	1½"
Bloom Lite	Pamphlet	39	Flower14	Layer	No	Green, yellow, orange, or blue patterned paper	1	1½"
Heritage	24	1	Leaves1	Shadow	Yes	Green cardstock	6	2"
Heritage cartridge	24	1	Leaves1	Shadow	Yes	Green patterned paper	6	1¾"
Home Accents Solutions	Pamphlet	2	Border1		No	Green cardstock	1	2"
Home Accents Solutions	Pamphlet	4	Border3		No	Green patterned paper	1	2"
Home Accents Solutions	Pamphlet	4	Border3		No	Green cardstock	1	2½"
Plantin Schoolbook	72	41	Circle	Shadow	No	Varied colors of patterned paper	10 (2 of each color)	¼"

Part 2: Assembly

1. Cut 8 squares of various-colored cardstock measuring 3" x 3".

2. Cut 8 squares of various-colored patterned paper measuring 3" x 3".

3. Round the corners of all 16 squares from steps 1 and 2 using a corner punch.

4. With a small dot of adhesive, adhere each square from steps 1 and 2 to a 12" x 12" piece of blue patterned cardstock.

5. Sew around the edges of the entire page layout with a straight stitch.

6. Sew a zigzag pattern straddling each row, moving top to bottom and left to right.

Note: Each square of paper should be sewn down on all 4 sides.

7. Ink around the edges of all die cuts as desired.

8. Assemble butterfly die cuts by attaching layer pieces to the base image.

9. Use a pencil to curl wing tips of top layer.

10. Adhere crystal gems to center of the butterflies to form the body.

11. Assemble "spring" banner with colored pieces over the white base banner piece.

12. Adhere banner to upper-left corner of layout.

13. Remove the leg portions of 2 small brads.

14. Adhere the head portion of the brads to each end of the banner die cut.

15. Assemble the layer and base image of the "Happy" die cut.

16. Adhere the "Happy" die cut just above the banner on the layout.

17. Ink the edges of each white frame with a blue inkpad.

18. Use half-back pearls or brads to secure the top of the 5 frames to the layout.

Note: For more dimension, each white frame can be embossed with a Cuttlebug using the D'Vine Swirls embossing folder. Pictures can be inserted in the frames from underneath.

19. Adhere border die cuts to the bottom edge of the layout.

20. Cut 5 strips of various-colored patterned paper measuring 1" x 12".

21. Accordion fold each strip of paper and adhere ends to each other.

22. Push down and hold together the center to create flower shape.

23. Using a strong adhesive, adhere a small circle to the top and bottom of each accordion flower to keep them flat.

24. Attach a die-cut flower to the top center of each flower.

25. Tie a piece of craft thread through the holes of each button.

26. Attach a button to the center of each accordion flower, as shown.

27. Ink the edges of each accordion flower with various-colored inkpads.

28. Attach accordion flowers to the bottom of the page layout.

29. Ink, curl, and crease leaf die cuts.

30. Attach leaves as desired around the base of all flowers.

31. Place layout in a shadow box frame.

32. Decorate the outside corners of the shadow box with the remaining butterflies and borders.

Autumn Glow

By Lisa Sheffield
Cricut Cuts: Advanced Level

MATERIALS

- Designer's Calendar Cartridge
- Winter Woodland Cartridge
- 15" wood baluster (can be purchased at a home improvement store)
- 4½" x 4½" x 1⅛" hardwood block molding (can be purchased at a home improvement store)
- 6-sided wood photo display cube
- 2 screws
- Brown acrylic paint
- Clear transparency film or clear contact paper
- Brown cardstock
- Green cardstock
- Craft wire
- Brown craft inkpad
- Clear adhesive
- 2.5-ounce votive candle

INSTRUCTIONS

Part 1: Wood Preparation

1. Draw an "x" on the bottom of the block molding.

2. Drill small hole in the center of the "x."

3. Screw a 1" screw through the base and into the thickest end of baluster.

Note: Make sure the baluster is straight and the screw sinks completely into the base.

4. Remove the glass and photo-backing material from the photo box.

5. Draw an "x" inside the bottom of the photo box.

6. Drill a small hole in the center of the marked "x."

7. Screw a 1" screw through the box base and into the opposite end of the baluster.

8. Paint all wood pieces.

9. Paint photo box inside and out (except the glass).

10. Measure and cut a piece of felt to attach to the bottom of the candle holder when the paint is dry.

Part 2: Cricut Die-Cut Pieces

Cartridge	Page #	Keypad #	Basic Key	Creative Feature Key	Shift	Paper Type	Qty.	Size
Designer's Calendar	36	9	Leaf	Boxed	Yes	Clear contact paper or transparency film	4	3"
Winter Woodland	57	26	Sqrrl-s		Yes	Green cardstock	3	2"
Winter Woodland	57	26	Sqrrl-s		Yes	Brown cardstock	3	2"

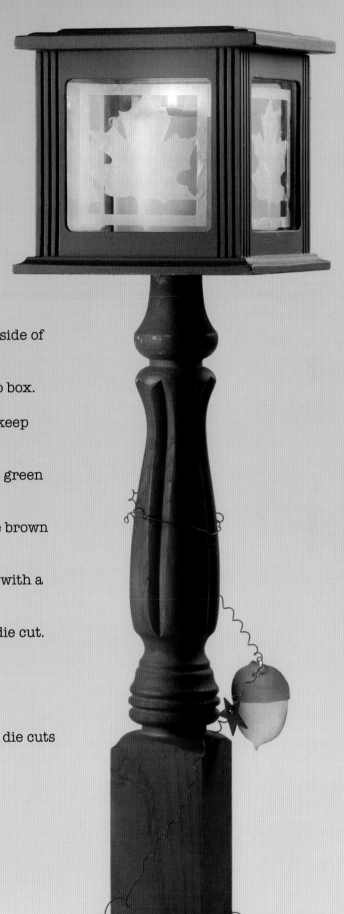

Part 3: Assembly

1. Apply a leaf to the center of each glass side of the photo box.

2. Reinsert the glass pieces into the photo box.

3. Use a clear adhesive in each corner to keep glass pieces in place.

4. Cut off the cap portion from all 3 of the green acorn die cuts.

5. Glue the green acorn caps on top of the brown acorn die cuts.

6. Ink the edges of each assembled acorn with a brown inkpad.

7. Punch hole through top of each acorn die cut.

8. Place wire through hole in each acorn.

9. Wrap wire around baluster.

Note: Use glue dots to hold wire and acorn die cuts in place

10. Place votive candle in the photo box.

GIFTS & PARTIES

Start Your Engines

Once Upon a Princess

Happily Ever After

I Heart the USA

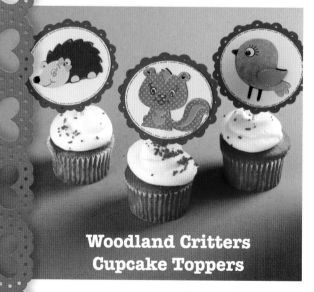

**Woodland Critters
Cupcake Toppers**

**Woodland Critters
Party Favor**

Cowboy Up!

Huntin' Season

Spooky Album

I Want My Mummy

Ready, Set, Hike

Parisian Bridal Shower

Start Your Engines

By Jenny Johnson
Cricut Cuts: Intermediate Level

MATERIALS

- Life's a Party Cartridge
- Boys Will Be Boys Cartridge
- Mini Monsters Cuttlebug Companion embossing folder
- Small scrapbook springs
- Craft paper
- Birthday sentiment
- Striped patterned paper
- Racing checker patterned paper

- Silver brads
- Yellow cardstock
- Black cardstock
- Black marker or pen
- White gel pen
- Black raffia
- Corner rounder punch
- Dimensional adhesive

INSTRUCTIONS

Part 1: Cricut Die-Cut Pieces

Note: Change Settings Unit to inches—$1/10$ths for these die cuts. For more information, see page 38.

Cartridge	Page #	Keypad #	Basic Key	Creative Feature Key	Shift	Paper Type	Qty.	Size
Life's a Party	56	36	MonkyHat		No	Racing checker patterned paper	1	8.80"
Life's a Party	66	46	WindwBox	Font	No	Yellow cardstock	1	1"
Life's a Party	66	46	WindwBox	Font Shadow	No	Black cardstock	1	1"
Boys Will Be Boys	68	41	RaceCar		No	Craft cardstock	3	3"
Boys Will Be Boys	68	41	RaceCar		Yes	Striped patterned paper	3	3"
Boys Will Be Boys	68	41	RaceCar	Layer	No	White cardstock	3	3"
Boys Will Be Boys	68	41	RaceCar	Layer	Yes	Black cardstock	1	3"
Boys Will Be Boys	68	41	RaceCar		No	Craft cardstock	2	1.40"
Boys Will Be Boys	68	41	RaceCar		Yes	Striped patterned paper	2	1.40"
Boys Will Be Boys	68	41	RaceCar	Layer	No	White cardstock	2	1.4"
Boys Will Be Boys	68	41	RaceCar	Layer	Yes	Black cardstock	2	1.40"

Part 2: Assembly

Party Hat

1. Assemble the hat, as shown.

2. Emboss larger black circle using the Mini Monsters Cuttlebug Companion embossing folder.

3. Assemble the 3" racecar and all layers.

4. Add silver brads to wheels on the racecar.

5. Add stitching to the racecar using a pen.

6. Adhere racecar and layers to the center front of the hat, with a spring.

Note: Use dimensional adhesive for the racecar.

zoomin' by with a birthday hi

7. Adhere the "birthday boy" title to the center front of the party hat.

8. Cut 3 triangles (about 2") each from the racing checker patterned paper and the yellow cardstock.

9. Layer racing patterned paper triangles on yellow cardstock triangles.

10. Adhere triangles to top of hat.

Note: Use the scraps used to die cut the hat for the triangles.

Card/Invitation

1. Cut a 4¼" x 11" piece of black cardstock and fold in half.

2. Cut a 4" x 5¼" piece of racing checker patterned paper.

3. Cut a 4¼" x 3" piece of yellow cardstock.

4. Round bottom corners of all layers.

5. Layer racing checker patterned paper and yellow cardstock.

6. Assemble racecar.

7. Adhere racecar to the card with a spring.

8. Add birthday sentiment to the bottom of the card.

9. Add black stitching around yellow mat and car parts.

Napkin Ring

1. Assemble smallest racecar.

2. Cut a 1¼" x 5¼" and a 2" x 2" piece of yellow cardstock.

3. Cut a 2" x 2" piece of racing checker patterned paper.

4. Emboss smaller black circle using the Mini Monsters Cuttlebug Companion embossing folder.

5. Adhere 2 ends of yellow strip together.

6. Assemble layers and racecar, as shown.

7. Add stitching to racecar with a pen.

8. Adhere racecar to the front of the ring with a spring.

Once Upon a Princess

By Jenny Johnson
Cricut Cuts: Beginner Level

MATERIALS

- Once Upon a Princess Cartridge
- Cloud patterned paper
- Cardstock (lime green, turquoise, white, flesh-colored, light pink, fuchsia, green glitter)
- Post-it Craft paper or other self-adhesive paper.
- Sentiment stamps

- Facial features stamp set
- Gems
- Popsicle or craft sticks
- White gel pen
- Gold glitter glue
- Adhesive
- Floral foam or Styrofoam

INSTRUCTIONS

Part 1: Cricut Die-Cut Pieces

Cartridge	Page #	Keypad #	Basic Key	Creative Feature Key	Shift	Paper Type	Qty.	Size
Once Upon a Princess	27	3	Doll3		No	Flesh-colored cardstock	1	3.80"
Once Upon a Princess	27	3	Doll3		Yes	Flesh-colored cardstock	1	3.80"
Once Upon a Princess	27	3	Doll3	Layer	No	Pink-colored cardstock	1	3.80"
Once Upon a Princess	73	47	Invite1		No	Fuchsia cardstock*	1	5.40"
Once Upon a Princess	68	45	Crown2		No	Fuchsia cardstock	1	3.0"
Once Upon a Princess	68	45	Crown2	Layer	No	Green glitter cardstock	1	3.0"
Once Upon a Princess	65	42	GiftBag2		No	Turquoise cardstock	1	6.90"
Once Upon a Princess	43	20	Pajamas	Tag	No	Fuchsia cardstock	1	2.50"
Once Upon a Princess	43	20	Pajamas	Tag	No	Fuchsia cardstock	1	2.0"
Once Upon a Princess	43	20	Pajamas	Tag	Yes	Lime green cardstock	1	2.0"
Once Upon a Princess	34	11	Dress2	Phrase	Yes	Fuchsia cardstock	1	3.40"
Once Upon a Princess	34	12	Dress3	Phrase	No	Lime green cardstock	1	1.5"
Once Upon a Princess	34	12	Dress3	Phrase	Yes	Turquoise cardstock	1 (use only the package tie)	1.5"
Once Upon a Princess	34	11	Dress3	Gem	No	Turquoise cardstock	1	2.50"
Once Upon a Princess	34	11	Dress3**	Gem	No	Lime green cardstock	1	2.50"

*Note: A strip of green glitter cardstock has been added behind the crown cuts.

**Note: Use the cake cutout that is taken out of this piece on the bag.

Part 2: Assembly

Invitation

1. Assemble all layers of the princess, as shown.

2. Fold the fuchsia card so the scalloped edge is in the front and "Princess Party" shows from the back, as shown.

3. Adhere a strip of green glitter cardstock behind the crown cuts.

4. Cut a 2¼" x 5" piece of cloud patterned paper.

5. Adhere the cloud paper to the card front.

6. Adhere assembled princess on top of cloud paper.

7. Stamp a "You're Invited" sentiment on the card front.

Crown

1. Adhere crown layers together.

2. Apply generous amount of gold glitter glue to the bottom crown layer.

3. Add gems to crown points.

Bag

1. Assemble bag.

2. Stamp the cake die cut with a facial features stamp.

3. Stamp sentiment on the small fuchsia tag piece.

4. Adhere to lime green cardstock tag and attach to the front of bag.

5. Add detailing with a white gel pen.

Happy Birthday Sign

1. Adhere "Happy Birthday" title to front of tag.

2. Adhere the package tie to the Happy Birthday Phrase.

3. Adhere a green jewel over the "i" for detail.

4. Adhere tag to craft stick.

Cake Sign

1. Adhere cake to lime green layer.

2. Stamp face onto front of the cake with a facial features stamp.

3. Stamp a sentiment under the cake.

4. Add glitter glue to the edge of the sign and on the cake candle.

5. Add a border with a white gel pen inside the glitter border.

6. Adhere sign to a craft stick.

Birthday Girl Sign

1. Cut star with reverse side of Post-it Craft paper, or any self-adhesive craft paper.

2. Apply generous amount of gold glitter to the adhesive side of the paper.

3. Adhere "Birthday Girl" die cut on top of the star.

4. Adhere sign to a craft stick.

Happily Ever After

By Paula Sanders
Cricut Cuts: Beginner Level

MATERIALS

- 11" x 17" frame
- Storybook Cartridge
- Sentimentals Cartridge
- Vinyl and transfer tape

- Etching cream
- Masking tape
- Gems (5 mm)
- Cardstock (black, white)

INSTRUCTIONS

Part 1: Cricut Die-Cut Pieces

Cartridge	Page #	Keypad #	Basic Key	Shift	Creative Feature Key	Function	Paper Type	Qty.	Size
Sentimentals	65	42	Card1	No			White cardstock	1	6"
Sentimentals	65	42	Card1	No			White cardstock	1	5"
Sentimentals	65	42	Card1	No			Black cardstock	1	5¼"
Storybook	57	4	Flourish3	Yes	Tall/Border		White cardstock	1	¾"
Storybook	69		EverAftr	No		Flip	Vinyl*	1	2½"
Storybook	Various	Various	1, 4, A, u, g, s, t, 2, 0, 0, 9**	Yes on A		Flip	Vinyl	1 of each	1"
Storybook	42	19	Heart	Yes			Vinyl	1	2½"

*Check the Cutting Guide on page 44 for the correct settings for vinyl.

**This is the date in the example, but you can change the date to the couple's names or a date of your choice.

Part 2: Assembly

1. Cut an 11" x 17" piece of black cardstock.

Note: Most scrapbook paper is 12" x 12", so you may need to look at non-scrapbook paper companies to find this size of cardstock. You can also use other papers, such as Japanese papers, which are normally larger than 12" x 12".

2. Lay background paper on table and arrange photo and paper embellishments, and decide where the etched portions (using the vinyl as a stencil) will go.

3. Cut around the outside of each vinyl design 1" to 2".

Note: For tips on working with vinyl, see page 28.

4. With the hook tool, remove the heart design, letters, and phrase "Happily Ever After" from the vinyl outline.

Note: Leave in the centers of the letters since the vinyl will be used as a stencil.

5. Cut a piece of transfer tape to fit the vinyl designs, and put the transfer tape on the vinyl.

6. Use the scraper tool to burnish all of the vinyl designs.

7. Apply vinyl designs to back side of the glass and tape around the edges.

Note: The letters and phrase were cut flipped and in reverse order, so they should read correctly from the front side of the glass. Make sure the words read correctly before using the etching cream.

8. Tape off all areas that you don't want etched.

9. Use a stick to apply the etching cream to the open spaces in the vinyl.

Note: Make sure the cream is applied thickly and covers all the areas completely.

10. Wait 10 minutes (or however long the instructions on the etching cream container indicate).

11. Scrape off all the cream and put it back in the cream container.

12. Rinse the etched glass under running water with a sponge or cloth.

13. Dry the glass and carefully pull off the tape and vinyl.

14. Put the etched glass into the frame.

15. Adhere die-cut pieces and wedding announcement to the background piece.

16. Insert background paper in the frame.

17. Add jewels to the front of the glass.

I Heart the USA

By Cathie Rigby
Cricut Cuts: Beginner Level

MATERIALS

- Independence Day Cartridge
- Denim tote
- Red, white, and blue cotton fabric
- Red puffy velvet fabric marker
- Iron-on adhesive
- Heat embossing tool
- Buttons
- Iron

INSTRUCTIONS

Part 1: Fabric Preparation

1. Cut an 8" x 8" section of cotton fabric.

2. Cut an 8" x 8" section of iron-on adhesive.

3. Iron the iron-on adhesive to the back of the fabric.

4. When the fabric is cool, remove the paper backing from the fabric and place the fabric on the Cricut cutting mat.

Part 2: Cricut Die-Cut Pieces

Note: Place the fabric opposite of Home Position, and using the directional arrows, move the blade to upper-right corner of the fabric, and use Set Paper Size button. For more information on Set Paper Size, see page 30.

Cartridge	Page #	Keypad #	Basic Key	Shift	Mode	Qty.	Size
Independence Day	Pamphlet	49	ILveUSA	No	Fit to Page	1	8"*

*Note: You don't need to set the size when using the Set Paper Size, but this is the size of the fabric being cut.

Part 3: Assembly

1. Iron die cut to the center of the bag, as shown.

Note: For iron-on tips, see page 181.

2. Use puffy velvet pen to highlight the outside edges of the saying.

3. Use heat embossing tool to create "puffy" effect.

4. Add buttons and embellishments, as desired.

Woodland Critters Cupcake Toppers

By Courtney Lee
Cricut Cuts: Beginner Level

MATERIALS

- Create a Critter Cartridge
- Cake Basics Cartridge
- Red cardstock
- Gray cardstock
- Black cardstock
- Ivory cardstock
- Pink cardstock
- Beige cardstock
- Blue patterned paper (with subtle pattern)
- Purple dot cardstock

- Peachy Keen Critter Faces stamps, large, #755
- Pink, black, and clear gems
- White gel pen
- Brown pen
- Black inkpad
- Adhesive
- Dimensional adhesive
- Toothpicks or short skewers

INSTRUCTIONS

Part 1: Cricut Die-Cut Pieces

Cartridge	Page #	Keypad #	Basic Key	Creative Feature Key	Shift	Paper Type	Qty.	Size
Cake Basics	36	9	Doily1		No	Red cardstock	6	3½"
Cake Basics	28	1	Circle	Base Shadow Blackout	No	Ivory cardstock	3	3½"
Create a Critter	62	39	Hedgehog		No	Black cardstock	1	1¾"
Create a Critter	62	39	Hedgehog	Layer1	No	Beige cardstock	1	1¾"
Create a Critter	62	39	Hedgehog	Layer2	No	Brown cardstock	1	1¾"
Create a Critter	62	39	Hedgehog	Layer3	No	Pink cardstock	1	1¾"
Create a Critter	61	38	Skunk		No	Black cardstock	1	2¼"
Create a Critter	61	38	Skunk	Layer1	No	Gray cardstock	1	2¼"
Create a Critter	61	38	Skunk	Layer2	No	Purple dot cardstock	1	2¼"
Create a Critter	45	22	Gator		Yes	Black cardstock	1	2¼"
Create a Critter	45	22	Gator	Layer1	Yes	Blue cardstock	1	2¼"
Create a Critter	45	22	Gator	Layer2	Yes	Gray cardstock	1	2¼"

Part 2: Assembly

1. Stamp faces onto the critters using a black inkpad.

2. Fill in the eyes with the white gel pen.

3. Assemble the layers of the hedgehog, bird, and skunk.

4. Use dimensional adhesive to adhere wing to the bird.

5. Adhere the ivory circles to the doily bases.

6. Use the brown pen to faux stitch around the edges of the ivory circles.

7. Adhere the critters to the circles using dimensional adhesive.

8. Use the white gel pen to doodle on the critters as desired.

9. Adhere a pink gem to the center of the bow on the hedgehog.

10. Adhere a second doily to back of each assembled doily with a toothpick or skewer in the middle of the doilies.

Woodland Critters Party Favor

By Courtney Lee
Cricut Cuts: Beginner Level

MATERIALS

Create a Critter Cartridge

Everyday Paper Dolls Cartridge

Red cardstock

White cardstock

Green cardstock

Woodgrain patterned paper

Yellow patterned paper (subtle pattern)

Character face stamps

White gel pen

Red grosgrain ribbon with a white stitch

Black inkpad

Adhesive

Dimensional adhesive

Toilet paper roll

Pink pen or pencil

Hot glue gun

INSTRUCTIONS

Part 1: Cricut Die-Cut Pieces

Cartridge	Page #	Keypad #	Basic Key	Creative Feature Key	Shift	Paper Type	Qty.	Size
Everyday Paper Dolls	69	42	Garden	Accessories1	Yes	Green cardstock	1	1¾"
Everyday Paper Dolls	69	42	Garden	Accessories1	Yes	Green cardstock	2	1¼"
Create a Critter	32	9	Squirrel		Yes	Yellow patterned paper	1	1½"
Create a Critter	32	9	Squirrel	Layer2	Yes	White cardstock	1	1½"
Create a Critter	32	9	Squirrel	Layer3	Yes	Red cardstock	1	1½"
Create a Critter	32	9	Squirrel		Yes	Yellow patterned paper	1	1"
Create a Critter	32	9	Squirrel	Layer2	Yes	White cardstock	1	1"
Create a Critter	32	9	Squirrel	Layer3	Yes	Red cardstock	1	1"

Part 2: Assembly

1. Stamp faces onto the mushrooms using the black ink.

2. Fill in the eyes with a white gel pen.

3. Assemble the mushroom layers.

4. Use dimensional adhesive to adhere the top of the mushroom to its base.

5. Add cheeks to the mushrooms with a pink pen or pencil.

6. Use the white gel pen to doodle on the mushrooms, as desired.

7. Cut a 6½" x 4½" piece of the woodgrain paper.

8. Adhere woodgrain paper around toilet paper roll, and secure.

9. Using the hot glue gun, adhere leaves and mushrooms to the top of the covered toilet paper roll.

10. Using the hot glue gun, adhere ribbon to the bottom of the toilet paper roll.

11. Bring ribbon around the sides of the toilet paper roll to hold in any candy or treats, and tie a bow.

Cowboy Up!

By Cathie Rigby
Cricut Cuts: Beginner to Intermediate Level

MATERIALS

For boy version:
- Red bandana cotton fabric print
- Black and red iron-on vinyl
- Puffy velvet fabric marker, black and red

For girl version:
- Pink bandana cotton fabric print
- Green and pink iron-on vinyl

For both versions:
- Paper Doll Dress Up Cartridge
- Old West Cartridge
- Infant shirt or bodysuit
- Iron-on adhesive
- Iron
- Heat embossing tool
- Puffy velvet pen
- Fabric adhesive
- Silver star sequins and half back pearls

INSTRUCTIONS

Part 1: Fabric Preparation

1. Cut a 8" x 8" section of cotton fabric.

2. Cut an equal amount of iron-on adhesive.

3. Iron the iron-on adhesive to the back of the fabric.

4. When the fabric is cool, remove the paper backing from fabric, and place on the Cricut cutting mat.

Part 2: Cricut Die-Cut Pieces

Cartridge	Page #	Keypad #	Basic Key	Shift	Creative Feature Key	Mode	Paper Type	Qty.	Size
Paper Doll Dress Up	66	38	Cowboy	No	Accessories 1	Real Dial Size	Red or pink bandana fabric	1	2½"
Old West	72		CowboyUp	No			Black or green iron-on vinyl	1	1½"
Old West	72		CwbyUp-s	Yes			Red or pink iron-on vinyl	1	1½"

Part 3: Assembly

1. Iron the die-cut boots to the center of the baby shirt.

2. Iron on the vinyl letter pieces.

3. Use a puffy velvet pen to highlight the outside edges of the boot.

4. Use a heat embossing tool to create a "puffy" effect.

5. Repeat steps 3–4 for the inner-boot details.

6. Decorate as you wish.

Iron-On Vinyl Tips

1. Iron-on vinyl should go on the cutting mat shiny side up, dull side down.

2. After the vinyl is cut, place it on the baby shirt where you want it to stay.

3. Iron the vinyl piece on the baby shirt on medium-high setting, with no steam.

4. After ironing, remove the shiny plastic layer from the image.

Note: The final image will be underneath this protective layer.

Huntin' Season

By Anne Burgess
Cricut Cuts: Intermediate Level

MATERIALS

- Accent Essentials Cartridge
- Wildlife Lite Cartridge
- Old West Cartridge
- Dark brown cardstock
- Light brown cardstock
- Wood grain patterned paper
- Tissue box
- Adhesive
- Twine or cording

INSTRUCTIONS

Part 1: Preparation

Tissue Box Sides

1. Cut two 5⅛" x 9½" pieces of light brown cardstock.

2. Score each piece from step 1 at ½" and 5", and fold on score lines.

3. Cut four 4¼" x 4" pieces of patterned paper.

4. Cut four 4¼" x ¾" pieces of patterned paper.

Tissue Box Top

5. Cut a 6⁹⁄₁₆" x 6⁹⁄₁₆" square of light brown cardstock.

6. Score the square at 1" on all sides, and fold on all score lines.

7. Cut along the right score line of each side to the next score line.

Note: Place this piece in the middle of the cutting mat when cutting it on the Cricut Expression.

8. Cut a 4¼" x 4¼" piece of patterned paper.

Note: Place this piece in the middle of the cutting mat when cutting it on the Cricut Expression.

Part 2: Cricut Die-Cut Pieces

Cartridge	Page #	Keypad #	Basic Key	Shift	Creative Feature Key	Mode	Function	Paper Type	Qty.	Size
Accent Essentials	79	48	Accent48	Yes		Center Point*		Brown cardstock from step 5 above	1	2¼"
Accent Essentials	79	48	Accent48	No		Center Point*		Patterned paper from step 8 above	1	2¼"
Wildlife	Pamphlet	38	Buck	No				Dark brown cardstock	1	3¾"
Wildlife	Pamphlet	3	Horns	No			Flip	Dark brown cardstock	1	3¾"
Wildlife	Pamphlet	31	Antlers	No				Dark brown cardstock	1	3¾"
Wildlife	Pamphlet			No				Dark brown cardstock	1	3¾"
Old West	42	19	"O"	No	Icon	Mix 'n Match	Flip one	Dark brown cardstock	2	1"

*Note: Place this piece in the middle of your cutting mat when you cut it on the machine.

Part 3: Assembly

1. Adhere the ½" folded sides of the pieces from step 1 on facing page to form box.

2. Adhere sides of piece from step 5 on facing page to create a lid.

3. Adhere all patterned paper to box sides and lid.

4. Wrap twine around box lid and tie knot in the front.

5. Adhere Cricut die cuts to all the sides.

Spooky Album

By Cathie Rigby
Cricut Cuts: Advanced Level

MATERIALS

- Mini Monsters Cartridge
- Robotz Font Cartridge
- Happy Hauntings Cartridge
- Gypsy Wanderings Cartridge
- From My Kitchen Cartridge
- Paper Doll Dress Up Cartridge
- Plantin Schoolbook Cartridge
- Chipboard
- 2 #10 white envelopes
- Dimensional adhesive
- Ribbon (green, purple)
- Bat, pumpkin ribbon
- Spider web, chain, and boo border punches
- Halloween patterned paper
- Halloween embossed paper
- Craft foam: turquoise and white glitter
- Your Story Laminating machine
- 6" x 6" laminating sheet
- Deep-cut blade
- Halloween image and sentiment stamps
- Half back black pearls
- Watermark or Embossing stamp pad
- Clear embossing powder
- Heating tool and tweezers
- Googly eyes
- Bloodshot eyes stickers
- Raffia, stapler, gel pen, black pen, and ink
- Cardstock

INSTRUCTIONS

Part 1: Cricut Die-Cut Pieces for Cover

Cartridge	Page #	Keypad #	Basic Key	Creative Feature Key	Shift	Function	Paper Type	Qty.	Size
Mini Monsters	71	44	Gravel	Base Shadow	No		Chipboard	4	7"
Mini Monsters	71	44	Gravel	Base Shadow	No	Flip (2)	Black cardstock	2, 2 flipped	7"
Mini Monsters	71	44	Gravel	Base Shadow	No		Orange, dark turquoise cardstock	2	7"
Mini Monsters	71	44	Gravel	Base Shadow	No		Flocked transparency material	1	7"
Mini Monsters	71	44	Gravel	Base Shadow	No	Flip (2)	Dark turquoise cardstock, dots, spider web patterned paper	2	7"
Gypsy Wanderings	Pamphlet	46	Skull		No		White cardstock	1	4.10"
Gypsy Wanderings	Pamphlet	46	Skull	Shadow	No		White cardstock	1	4.10"
Robotz Font	49 47 46 55 43	22 20 19 28 16	S, P, O, O, K, Y	Blackboard	Yes		White cardstock	1	1½"

Part 2: Assembly

1. Cut 1" x ½" white cardstock and score and fold in half to create tab.

2. Adhere tab to the top back side of skull and top front side of the shadow skull to create a card. Trim edges where necessary.

3. Cut black cardstock to fit the cover of the album, and adhere it to the chipboard coffin die cut.

4. Adhere letters to the mouth of skull piece.

Note: Cricut Craft Room users can weld letters to be part of the skull piece.

5. Cut bone patterned paper to 3" x 3¾" and adhere behind the skull card front, as shown.

6. Add stitch marks with white gel pen around the bone patterned paper.

Part 3: Cricut Die-Cut Pieces for Pages 1 and 2

Cartridge	Page #	Keypad #	Basic Key	Creative Feature Key	Shift	Function	Paper Type	Qty.	Size
Happy Hauntings	40	13	Frame3-s		Yes		Purple embossed paper	1	5½"
Happy Hauntings	40	13	Frame3-s		Yes	Flip	Purple embossed paper	1	5½"
Happy Hauntings	40	13	Frame3		No		Purple embossed paper	1	5½"
Mini Monsters	70	43	StrtSign		No	Flip	Black cardstock	1	6"
From My Kitchen	37	10	Frame3-s	Tabs	No		Orange cardstock	1	3.3"

Part 4: Assembly

1. Adhere dark turquoise coffin die cuts to chipboard album pages 1 and 2.

2. Adhere frame die cuts with no opening to each other, creating a pocket opening on the left side for tag.

3. Stamp Halloween sentiment to top of page 1 twice with white ink.

4. When the white ink is dry, stamp the sentiment with black ink for a shadowed effect.

5. Remove bat images from top and bottom of the frame die cut with the window.

6. Laminate the frame die cut with a window using the Your Story machine or other laminating machine.

7. Trim excess laminating material away from frame when cool.

8. Cut a ¾" x 5" piece of silver cardstock and punch with a chain-link border punch.

9. Cut the chain-link piece into 2 equal pieces, and fold each piece in half.

10. Place the laminated window over the pocket die cut, and glue the chain to the front and back of the right side to create a hinge, as shown.

11. Adhere entire frame piece to page 1.

12. Use the leftover window insert to trace a pattern on white cardstock.

13. Cut out the pattern and fold it into thirds to create a trifold journaling block.

14. Stamp a sentiment on the front piece and insert inside frame pocket on page 1.

15. Cut a 2¾" x 3½" piece of trick-or-treater patterned paper to create a photo mat.

16. Adhere the photo mat from part 4, step 15 to page 2 using dimensional adhesive.

Note: Do not adhere the top side of the photo mat to create a pocket.

17. Use a scrap piece of yellow glitter cardstock to place behind the opening on the street lamp die cut.

18. Adhere the street lamp die cut to the right side of photo mat on page 2.

Note: Make sure the arm of the lamp goes across photo mat in a way that allows the pocket from the photo mat to remain open.

19. Cut a 2¼" x 3¾" piece of spider patterned paper and insert into pocket.

20. Stamp a sentiment on the orange tab and attach to the spider patterned paper insert.

21. Adhere cut bats to top of page 2.

22. Add details to the street lamp with a white gel pen.

Part 5: Cricut Die-Cut Pieces for Pages 3 and 4

Cartridge	Page #	Keypad #	Basic Key	Creative Feature Key	Shift	Mode	Paper Type	Qty.	Size
Paper Doll Dress Up	49	21	Cstume-s	Accessories2, Real Dial Size	Yes		Black cardstock	1	4¾"
Paper Doll Dress Up	49	21	Cstume	Accessories2, Real Dial Size	No		Turquoise craft foam*	1	1½"
Paper Doll Dress Up	49	21	Cstume-s	Accessories1, Real Dial Size	Yes		White glitter craft foam*	1	3"
Paper Doll Dress Up	49	21	Cstume-s	Accessories1, Real Dial Size	Yes		White glitter craft foam*	1	3½"
Plantin Schoolbook	69		Grass		Yes	Fit to Length	Green cardstock	1	4"
Happy Hauntings	62	35	Grvyrd-s	Spooky Font, Real Dial Size	Yes		Dark turquoise cardstock	1	¾"
Happy Hauntings	46	19	Frame9-s	Spooky Font, Real Dial Size	Yes		Dark turquoise cardstock	2	¾"

*Note: Use a deep-cut blade on this cut, if possible.

Tip: When cutting foam, the machine's roller can add indentations to the foam. You can either flip the image on your cut so the reverse side does not have indentations or you can iron out the creases by rubbing your bone folder across the back portion of the image.

Part 6: Page 3 Assembly

1. Adhere black coffin die cuts to chipboard album pages 3 and 4.

2. Cut spider web patterned paper coffin die diagonally across the top to create a large pocket, as shown.

3. Cut a 5¼" x 2" piece of green cardstock.

4. Use a spider web border punch on 1 edge of the green cardstock.

5. Adhere spider web piece to the top of the spider patterned paper.

6. Wrap sheer green ribbon around entire coffin pocket and tie knot in the front.

7. Adhere assembled spider patterned paper pocket to page 3 with dimensional adhesive, and leave the top open to create a pocket.

8. Stamp a Halloween sentiment on a scrap piece of orange cardstock.

9. Trim sentiment, and adhere it under the ribbon knot.

10. Using a black pen, add details to the blue foam spider.

11. Stamp foam spider and spider web die cuts with watermark inkpad in random manner and sprinkle with clear embossing powder.

12. Use tweezers to hold die-cut spider, and apply heat with a heating tool to slightly warp legs of the spider and to create texture over entire shape.

Note: Foam can burn and yellow if it gets too hot, so use caution, and use small bursts of heat.

13. Adhere spider web to the bottom of the pocket on page 3.

14. When the foam is cool, attach googly eyes to the spider and adhere the spider to the center of the web with dimensional adhesive.

15. Cut a 3¼" x 6½" piece of purple cardstock.

16. Cut two 3" x 3" pieces of white patterned paper, and ink the edges of both.

17. Cut a slit ½" down from the top on 1 white piece before adhering to purple cardstock.

18. Adhere both white pieces to purple cardstock with the slit piece at the top.

19. Insert bloodshot eyes stickers under the slit at the top, curling and tearing paper around the sides for dimension.

20. Insert the purple and white tag into pocket on page 3.

Part 7: Page 4 Assembly

1. Seal the top flaps of 2 white #10 envelopes.

2. Cut the right side of 1 envelope at the 8" mark on a paper trimmer (should remove approximately 1½").

3. Cut the left side of the second envelope at the 8" mark.

4. Cut along the bottom of each envelope to have the height equal 4".

Note: Less than an ⅛" will be removed to create an opening.

5. Score envelopes at 4" and fold so the sealed opening is on the outside of the fold.

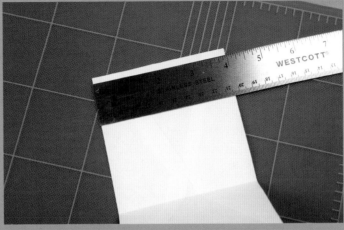

6. Lay envelope 1 (with the cut on the right end) vertically on the table. The upper long open slit should be on the right.

7. Lay envelope 2 (with the cut end on the left) horizontally over the other envelope. The open slit should be at the top.

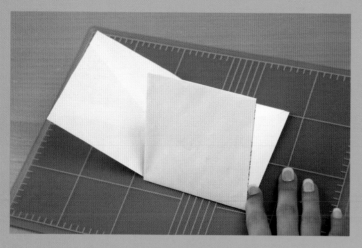

8. Fold up the bottom of envelope 1 to create a square.

9. Fold over envelope 2 to finish the square.

10. Adhere the entire square to the center of page 4.

11. Adhere envelope 2 to the top of envelope 1.

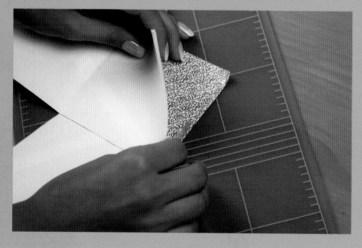

12. Seal the right side of both envelopes where they meet to create pockets in each envelope.

Tip: Use ⅛"-thick double-sided tape. There should now be 3 inside squares and 2 outside squares for pictures. There should be 2 openings at the top for tags and one opening on the flap that opens downward.

13. Cut three 3¾" x 3¾" pieces of black spider patterned paper.

14. Cut a 3¾" x 3¾" piece of black cardstock.

15. Adhere squares from part 7, steps 12 and 13 to the inside flaps of the envelope pages.

16. Tear a thin scrap piece of spider patterned paper and attach to the black square.

17. Cut a 3½" x 3½" piece of orange cardstock.

18. Cut a 3⅝" x 3⅝" piece of black cardstock.

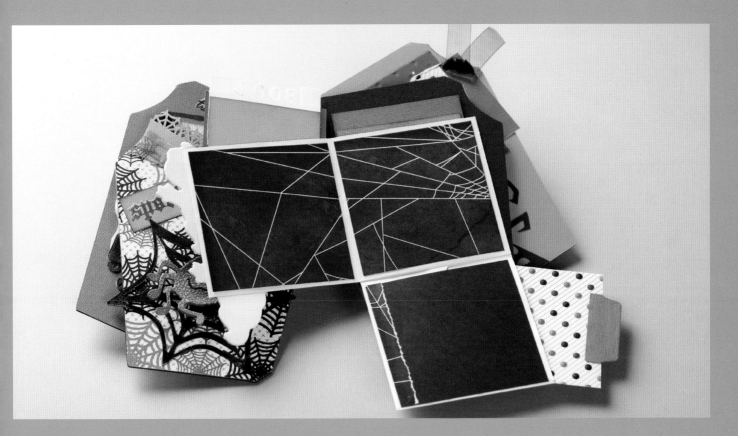

19. Attach the orange square to the black square and adhere to the front envelope flap, as shown.

20. Add half-back pearls to ghost die cuts for eyes, and use a black marker to accent detail lines.

21. Adhere the ghosts to right edge of the orange square, as shown.

22. Adhere grass to the bottom of page 4 and trim edges off.

23. Adhere blue "BOO" letters above grass, and add details with a white gel pen.

24. For the Boo tag, cut a 3¼" x 4" piece of purple cardstock.

25. Cut two 3" x 2" pieces of white cardstock.

26. Punch both white squares with the Martha Stewart BOO punch centered over the top.

27. Flip 1 white square and adhere to the back of other square with the purple square sandwiched in between to create a sturdier punched image.

28. Cut a 3" x 3¾" piece of trick-or-treater patterned paper, and adhere it to top of the tag, as shown.

29. Cut a 3" x 3¾" piece of orange paper, and adhere it to back of the tag from part 7, step 27.

30. Insert the tag in the front pocket.

31. For the RIP tag, cut a 3½" x 4" piece of purple cardstock, and adhere the RIP die cut to the front of the cardstock.

32. Insert the tab in the back pocket.

33. For the side-pocket tag, cut a 3½" x 4¼" piece of white-with-colored-dots patterned paper.

34. Cut a 3¼" x 4" piece of orange cardstock, and adhere to the back of tag from part 7, step 31.

35. Stamp a Halloween image on the left corner of the tag.

36. Attach the tab die cut to the right side of the tag, and insert the tag in the side pocket.

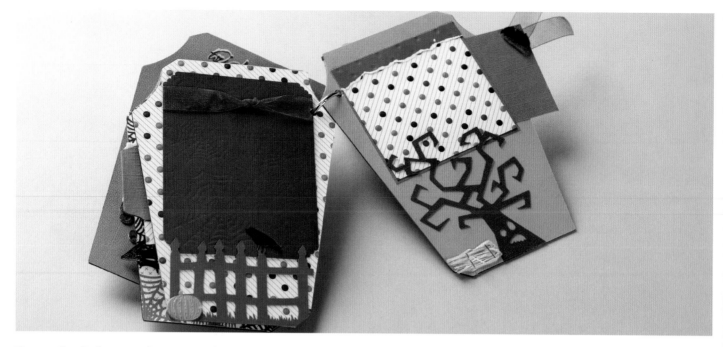

Part 8: Cricut Die-Cut Pieces for Pages 5 and 6

Cartridge	Page #	Keypad #	Basic Key	Creative Feature Key	Shift	Function	Paper Type	Qty.	Size
Happy Hauntings	66	39	Fence		No		Green cardstock	1	2½"
Happy Hauntings	66	39	Fence	Layer 2	No		Black cardstock	1	2½"
Happy Hauntings	67	40	Tree-s		Yes	Flip	Brown cardstock	1	4"

Part 9: Assembly

1. Adhere dotted patterned paper coffin die cut to page 5 of the chipboard album.

2. Cut a 3" x 5" piece of purple embossed paper and round the edges with cloud punch.

3. Tie a purple ribbon around top of the photo mat from step 2 and adhere to page 5.

4. Adhere fence die cut and black crow die cut to the bottom of page 5.

5. Adhere a pumpkin embellishment to the lower-left corner of page 5.

6. Adhere orange cardstock coffin die cut to page 6 of the chipboard album.

7. Cut a 3½" x 3¾" piece of dot-patterned paper.

8. Cut a 3⅝" x 3⅞" piece of purple cardstock.

9. Adhere dotted paper to purple square, leaving the right side open to create a pocket on the right side.

10. Adhere the pocket to the top of page 6.

11. Cut a 1" x 3½" piece of turquoise paper and tear 1 long edge.

12. Adhere the torn strip to the top of the pocket.

13. Adhere tree die cut to the bottom of page 6.

Note: Do not add glue behind the top branches so you can place a picture behind the branches on the photo mat.

14. Staple pieces of raffia to the lower left of tree base.

15. Create a tag for the pocket by cutting a 2¾" x 4" piece of purple cardstock.

16. Attach purple sheer ribbon to the upper corner and place a bat embellishment over ribbon.

I Want My Mummy

By Gayle Lambert
Cricut Cuts: Advanced Level

MATERIALS

- Mini Monsters Cartridge
- Heavy-duty fusible webbing
- 2 black buttons
- Black thread
- 13" x 15" black fabric piece
- 8" x 11" turquoise fabric piece
- 11" x 11" purple fabric piece
- 8" x 11" white fabric piece
- 12" wide green fabric
- 3" x 44" black polka dot fabric
- 3" x 44" orange fabric
- 3" x 58" strip of Halloween fabric for piping
- $1\frac{3}{4}$ yd $\frac{3}{8}$" cotton piping or pre-made piping
- 1 bag polyester stuffing

INSTRUCTIONS

Part 1: Fabric Preparation

1. Cut a 10" x 12" piece of green fabric.

2. Cut two $2\frac{1}{2}$" x 9" black polka dot fabric strips.

3. Cut two $2\frac{1}{2}$" x 11" black polka dot fabric strips.

4. Cut four $2\frac{1}{2}$" x $2\frac{1}{2}$" pieces of orange fabric.

5. Cut a $1\frac{3}{4}$" yards x 2" piece of Halloween fabric for piping, if you are making your own.

6. Cut heavy-duty fusible webbing for the turquoise, blue, and white fabric pieces.

7. Iron the fusible webbing to the back of the turquoise, blue, and white fabric pieces, according to webbing instructions.

8. When the fabric is cool, remove the paper backing from fabric piece before placing on cutting mat.

9. Place fabric onto clean and sticky cutting mat with the fabric side up.

10. Tape edges onto mat, if desired, to prevent fabric from moving before cutting.

Part 2: Cricut Die-Cut Pieces

Cartridge	Page #	Keypad #	Basic Key	Shift	Creative Feature Key	Paper Type	Qty.	Size
Mini Monsters	35	8	Mummy	No		Purple fabric	1	8"
Mini Monsters	36	8	Mummy	No	Layer 1	Turquoise fabric	1	8"
Mini Monsters	36	8	Mummy	Yes	Layer 1	White fabric	1	8"

Part 3: Assembly

Mummy

1. Take white bandage pieces from die cuts and layer onto turquoise body piece of mummy.

2. Take turquoise body piece and layer on purple body outline.

3. Iron all pieces in place being careful to have release paper backing under purple fabric so it does not stick to ironing board.

4. Iron on the layered mummy in the center of the green rectangle fabric piece.

5. When fabric is cool, top stitch the details of the mummy with a blanket stitch in black thread.

6. Iron entire fabric piece.

7. Sew on black buttons for eyes.

Pillow

Note: All seams are $\frac{1}{4}$".

1. Trim green rectangle to 9" x 11".

Note: Do not cut off the mummy's feet. Leave $\frac{1}{4}$" of green fabric beneath the feet.

2. Sew 9" x 2½" strips to the top and bottom of the green rectangle.

3. Sew 2½" orange squares to the ends of the 11" x 2½" strips.

4. Sew strips from part 1, step 3 to the sides of green rectangle, matching seams.

5. Prepare piping or use pre-made piping and sew onto pillow front $\frac{1}{4}$" from the edge.

Tip: If necessary, clip the piping to go around the corners easier.

6. Overlap the 2 ends of the piping.

7. With right sides together, sew pillow front and back together, leaving a 3" opening.

8. Turn pillow right side out and stuff with polyester stuffing.

9. Hand-stitch closed the remaining 3" opening.

Ready-Set-Hike

By Wendy Fellows
Cricut Cuts: Advanced Level

MATERIALS

- Campin' Critters Cartridge
- 12" x 12" denim fabric
- 12" x 12" Cricut stencil material
- Four 8" x 8" cotton fabric squares (red, yellow, green, aqua)
- Heavyweight fusible webbing
- Fine-point permanent marker or fabric marker
- Scissors
- Iron
- Deep-cut blade

- Hot-glue gun
- Glue sticks
- Painters tape
- Quilt or head pin

Try filling the backpack with some of these outdoor-themed items:

- Gift card to a sportsman's supply store
- Postage for letters home from camp
- Granola or trail mix in a plastic bag
- Small box of matches or flint stone
- Mini gel pen and mini notepad
- Mini flashlight
- Mini tissue packet
- Small compass
- Lip balm
- Candy
- Hand sanitizer

INSTRUCTIONS

Part 1: Prepare Cotton Fabric for Cutting

1. Iron fusible webbing onto the back side of the 8" x 8" cotton fabric squares.

2. When the fabric is cool to the touch, remove the paper backing from the back of webbing.

Note: If the paper does not easily come off the back of the fabric, then it has not been applied correctly and needs to be reheated.

Tip: It is best to not move the iron in a side-to-side motion. Instead, place the iron on the fabric for 8 seconds, and then pick the iron up and place it down on another section. This ensures that each section has enough direct heat applied to bond to the fabric.

Part 2: Prepare Reusable Stencil

1. Place 12" x 12" piece of the stencil material on the cutting mat.

2. Add painter's tape to the top and sides of material to hold the product firmly in place when cutting.

3. Remove regular blade housing and replace it with the deep-cut blade.

Note: The stencil material will require a multi cut function setting. See the cutting guide on page 44 for the exact settings to use for this material.

4. Cut the template using the Cricut Expression.

Note: This stencil can be used again and again to create this pattern.

Part 3: Cricut Die-Cut Pieces

Cartridge	Page #	Keypad #	Basic Key	Creative Feature Key	Shift	Mode	Paper Type	Qty.	Size
Campin' Critters	69	49	Backpack		No	Fit to Page	Cricut stencil material	1	10½"
Campin' Critters	69	49	BckPck-s		Yes		Red fused cotton fabric	1	10½"
Campin' Critters	69	49	Backpack	Layer1	No		Yellow fused cotton fabric	1	10½"
Campin' Critters	69	49	BckPck-s	Layer1	Yes		Green fused cotton fabric	1	10½"
Campin' Critters	69	49	Backpack	Layer2	No		Aqua fused cotton fabric	1	10½"

Part 4: Assembly

1. Remove backing from stencil material.

2. Attach stencil to the back of the denim fabric.

3. Trace the image using a marker.

4. Cut out the backpack base image with scissors.

5. Turn to Campin' Critters cartridge handbook page 73 for assembly instructions for all die-cut pieces.

6. Use hot glue to adhere the fabric together as liquid glues will not set up as quickly as needed.

Tip: Use a dress or quilt pin to spread glue evenly before it cools.

Parisian Bridal Shower

By Courtney Lee
Cricut Cuts: Advanced Level

MATERIALS

- French Manor Cartridge
- Tie the Knot Cartridge
- Elegant Cakes Cartridge
- Cuttlebug embosser
- Swiss Dots Cuttlebug Emboss Folder
- Patterned cardstock (brown, light blue, dark blue, cream stripe, cream damask, cream dot, white with brown design and dot)
- Plain cardstock (pink)
- White glittered cardstock
- Letter stamps
- Navy blue inkpad
- Badge pins
- Hot glue gun
- Eyelets
- Adhesive
- Ribbon (cream, dark brown)
- Dimensional adhesive

INSTRUCTIONS

Part 1: Cricut Die-Cut Pie

Cartridge	Page #	Keypad #	Basic Key	Shift	Creative Feature Key	Mode	Function	Paper Type	Qty.	Size
French Manor	68	41	EifflTwr	No	Card2			Dark blue patterned cardstock	1	2½"
French Manor	68	41	EifflTwr	Yes	Card2			Pink cardstock	1	2½"
French Manor	48	25	Victoria	No	Tag2			Brown patterned cardstock	1	2"
French Manor	48	25	Victoria	Yes	Tag2			Cream damask cardstock	1	2"
Tie the Knot	67	44	CakeBox	No		Fit to Page		Cream striped cardstock	1	12" x 12"*
Tie the Knot	67	44	Cake-Box-s	Yes		Fit to Page		Dark blue patterned cardstock	1	12" x 12"*
French Manor	76	49	Merci	No				White glitter cardstock	1	1¾"
French Manor	43	16	Cardinal	No	Layer			Light blue patterned cardstock	2	6¼"
French Manor	43	16	Cardinal	No	Layer		Flip	Cream dot patterned cardstock	2	6¼"
Elegant Cakes	28, 29	1, 2	Accent1, Accent2	No				Light blue patterned cardstock	1 of each number	¾"
Tie the Knot	65	42	Banner	No				Dark blue patterned cardstock	2	5"
Tie the Knot	65	42	Banner-s	Yes				Dark blue patterned cardstock	3	5"

Cartridge	Page #	Keypad #	Basic Key	Shift	Creative Feature Key	Paper Type	Qty.	Size
Tie the Knot	65	42	Banner-s	Yes		Striped cream patterned cardstock	2	5"
French Manor	66	39	FlrLs2	No		Brown patterned cardstock	1	5½"
French Manor	66	39	FlrLs2	No	Layer	Pink cardstock	1	5½"
French Manor	68	41	EifflTwr	No		Brown patterned cardstock	1	6"
French Manor	68	41	EifflTwr	No	Layer	Pink cardstock	1	6"
Tie the Knot	62	39	Mr&Mrs	No		White glitter cardstock	1	2"
Tie the Knot	62	39	Mr&Mrs	No	Blackout/Shadow	Brown patterned cardstock	1	2"
Tie the Knot	62	39	Mr&Mrs	No	Monogram	White glitter cardstock	1	2"
Tie the Knot	62	39	Mr&Mrs	No	Monogram Shadow	Brown patterned cardstock	1	2"
French Manor	49	22	Eleanor	No	Card1	Light blue patterned cardstock	1	5½"
French Manor	49	22	Eleanor	Yes	Card1	Cream damask patterned cardstock	1	5½"
French Manor	48		Victoria	No	Card1	White with brown design and dot patterned cardstock	1	5½"
French Manor	48		Victoria	Yes	Card1	Brown patterned cardstock	1	5½"

*Note: Turn off the Real Dial Size option for this cut.

Part 2: Assembly

Name Place Card

1. Fold dark blue cardstock card in half.

2. Stamp the name on the pink cardstock piece with navy ink.

3. Adhere pink cardstock so it shows through the front of the card.

4. Tie a dark brown ribbon around the front of the card, with a knot in the front.

Name Tag

1. Stamp the name with navy ink on the oval cream damask piece.

2. Layer the cream piece under the dark brown oval piece.

3. Attach a badge pin to the back of the tag with hot glue.

Favor Box

1. Fold all edges of the box so it forms a triangle-shaped box.

2. Adhere all tabs to assemble the box.

3. Fold and assemble the box lid the same as the box.

4. Adhere "Merci" to the box lid.

5. Thread dark brown ribbon through the holes in the box lid.

Table Numbers

1. Adhere numbers to the cream dot bird die cuts.

2. Adhere bamboo skewers between a cream bird and a light blue bird.

Note: Use hot glue to adhere the paper to the skewers and normal adhesive to adhere the tops of the birds.

Banner

1. Assemble brown and pink Eiffel Tower image.

2. Emboss the pink fleur-de-lis in a Cuttlebug using the Swiss Dots embossing folder.

3. Assemble the brown and pink fleur-de-lis.

4. Cut and discard the "&" from both "Mr. & Mrs." pieces.

5. Layer the glitter and brown pieces for "Mr," "&," and "Mrs."

6. Layer cream striped banner pieces on top of the dark blue scalloped pieces.

7. Add "Mr" and "Mrs" pieces to the banner pieces in part 2, step 6 with dimensional adhesive.

8. On the straight-edge blue banner pieces, add the Eiffel Tower, "&," and fleur-de-lis pieces with dimensional adhesive.

9. Add eyelets to the upper corners of each banner piece.

10. String cream ribbon through each eyelet.

Invitation

1. Fold light blue cardstock card in half.

2. Adhere cream damask cardstock so it shows through the front of the card.

3. Tie cream ribbon around the top portion of the card, as shown, and tie the ends in a bow.

Thank-You Card

1. Fold white and brown cardstock card in half.

2. Adhere 2 brown ribbons to front of card and adhere ends to the inside of the card.

3. Adhere brown cardstock with dimensional adhesive so it shows through the front of the card.

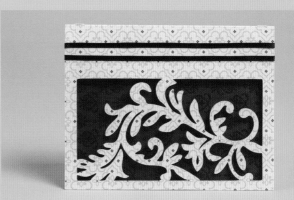

Glossary of Terms

Apply All
This feature of the Cricut Expression 2 machine allows users to edit all the images on the Cricut mat at the same time. It controls size, flip, rotation, and scale of the images on 1 screen.

Blackout
This is usually found as a creative feature key and allows users to cut a character without any detail markings. For example, if a user cut a letter "A," the machine would cut only an outline and not the small triangular piece in the center. For a character such as a paper doll, the blackout version of the cut would eliminate the facial details. Using this feature allows some creative license to stamp images or use rub-ons for added creativity.

Blade Assembly
The metal or plastic holder for the machine's blade is the blade assembly. The standard color has been green, but this has recently changed to coordinate with the different color options now available for Cricut Expression machines.

Burnish
A Cricut scraper can be used to apply pressure and create friction to, or burnish, the back side of a vinyl project. This allows the vinyl to easily move from the backing paper it came with to the transfer tape used to place an image on another surface.

Creative Feature Keys
These are the top 6 grey keys found on the left of the Cricut keypad. They are unique to each cartridge and are explained in the handbook. Not all cartridges have Creative Feature keys. When not available, the keypad will have a blank grey button and the handbook will indicate "Not Available" in different box selections.

Cricut Color Inks
More commonly referred to as Cricut Markers, these small markers are specially designed to fit in place of the blade assembly in a Cricut Expression. With these markers, users can create their own lined images in various color options. Marker lines can also be combined with a cut for a more defined look.

Cricut Craft Room
Cricut Craft Room is a free online design tool that allows users to access the entire Cricut Image Library. Mac and PC users can access the craft room through the Internet, and Cricut Expression 2 users with a WiFi adaptor can access wirelessly. This is the only way to purchase and use digital cartridges from Provo Craft.

Cricut DesignStudio
Cricut DesignStudio is a software product that allows users to connect their Cricut machines to their computers through a USB cable. The software makes it possible to see the entire Cricut Cartridge Library, manipulate characters from the cartridges with a virtual mat, weld various characters to create continuous phrases or images, and save created designs to a computer. Even though all images are available to view and manipulate, users can send an item to cut on their machines only if they own the physical cartridge the image appears on.

Crop

A scrapbooking event where people gather to work on their projects is known as a Crop. It is a social atmosphere usually scheduled in advance to allow crafters some designated time for card making or scrapbooking.

Cuttables

Cuttables are any products that can be cut with a Cricut Expression. Provo Craft has created a line of materials that it sells in many craft stores along with other Cricut products. However, there are many more items that can be cut with a Cricut machine available in various craft stores, so this term has a much broader reach than just the Provo Craft products.

Cutting Area Light

The light underneath the cradle arms of the Cricut Expression 2 blade assembly. This allows the cuts being made by the Cricut machine to be easily visible, even at night.

Cuttlebug

This die-cutting and embossing machine is produced by Provo Craft. It can be used with its own line of dies and embossing folders or with other compatible dies and folders. This is a manual system that includes cutting plates to allow for various thicknesses in dies.

Distressing

Distressing describes various methods of manipulating paper to give it an aged look. These include but are not limited to sanding, tearing, inking, painting, crumpling paper, and even using razor-edged tools to break up the paper. The goal with distressing is to create depth and texture and is consistent with particular design styles in scrapbooking.

Embossing

Embossing is a crafting technique that allows crafters to put a raised or depressed image or pattern on paper and other crafting materials. The technique can be a wet or dry process.

Fussy Cut

Using fine-point scissors to cut out small images from patterned paper to use separately as an embellishment on any paper-crafting project is called fussy cut.

Home

On the Cricut Expression 2 machine, this is the button that returns users to the home screen or main page. The machine's virtual mat, image selection button, and settings buttons are located here.

Home Position

This is the default starting point for the Cricut blade. On the Cricut Expression, it is located in the upper-right corner of the cutting mat. This is the spot directly under the Cricut blade when the machine is first turned on. On the Cricut Expression 2, Home Position is located in the upper-left corner of the cutting mat.

Image Spacing

This is the ability to control the amount of space between shapes and/or letters on a mat. This is a new feature available on the Cricut Expression 2 machine and is done by editing the space and line return buttons. Crafters can designate an exact measurement for each space or line return to control position of images on a Cricut mat.

Independent Image Sizing

This feature is available on the Cricut Expression 2 machine and allows multiple sizes to be cut on the same mat.

Inking

Inking is a crafting technique that applies ink from an inkpad to the edge of paper. The desired effect is to achieve a look that is worn, aged, or vintage in style. It creates dimension and texture and is commonly used as part of distressing paper.

Layer View

Layer view gives users the ability to see all of the creative layers of an image on the display screen at the same time.

LCD Touch Screen

This Cricut Expression 2 display screen shows color and replaces the cartridge keypad.

Mat Preview

A new feature available on the Cricut Expression 2 machine, Mat Preview allows crafters to see exactly where on the mat an image will be cut. This makes paper placement and cut accuracy optimal.

Materials

The Cricut Expression 2 allows crafters to define and save profiles for commonly used materials that the machine can cut.

Material Setting

This is the default settings for commonly used materials. On the Cricut Expression 2, there are preset material settings users can select from, or they can customize the settings wanted for the materials frequently used.

Multi Cut

Multi Cut refers to the number of passes the blade will make over the same character or image. A Cricut Expression can repeat the cut 2, 3, or 4 times in order to work through thicker material. Some Cricut Consumables require multiple passes for successful cutting.

Multiple Mat Cutting

A new feature of the Cricut Expression 2 machine, this allows cutting of large numbers of images even when they don't fit on 1 mat. The machine automatically prompts users to load the next mat when one is filled.

Release Cut

Release Cut is a small cut made perpendicular to a Cricut character that allows pressure to be put on 1 spot to snap the image away from the rest of the product. This technique is used on magnet material, craft foam, and transparency material.

Shadow

This is a very common creative feature on many Cricut cartridges. A shadow is a thicker version of a letter or shape and will cut proportionately larger than the original character.

Silhouette

A silhouette is a creative feature offered on some cartridges that will cut a thin outline of a character. It can usually be used on a base layer to accent a shape.

Welding

Welding is a term used to indicate letters or images are joined together as 1 continuous image. Crafters can take individual letters and weld them to cut as 1 piece. This can be done with any image or font-style letter.

Word Wrapping

Word wrapping is an automatic feature on the Cricut Expression that continues cutting on a new line after 1 line on the mat is filled with cut characters.

Work Area

The work area is the unshaded part of the mat preview screen. After setting the paper size, there will be only 1 section of the virtual mat where users can insert images for cutting.

CREATIVE CUTTING INSPIRATION

For more Cricut projects, instruction, inspiration, and fun, visit some of these creative Cricut users.

Bits of Paper
jamielanedesigns.blogspot.com

BugBites
bugbites411.blogspot.com

Cards by CG: Designs by Cheryl Gaffney
cardsbycg.blogspot.com

Cardz TV
cardztv.blogspot.com

Carson's Creations
carsonscricutcreations.blogspot.com

Cindy's Scraptastic Designs
cindybcreations.blogspot.com

Court's Crafts
courtscrafts.blogspot.com

Craft Junkie Too
www.craftjunkietoo.com

Crafting with Christina
craftingwithcristina.com

Crafting with Katie
craftingwithkatie.com

Crafty Chics
craftychicsblog.blogspot.com

Crazy about Cricut
crazyaboutcricut.blogspot.com

Crazy Card Creator
crazycardcreator.blogspot.com

Create with Expression
expressionbypinke.blogspot.com

Creative Cutter Room
www.creativecutterroom.com

Cricut Couple
cricutcouple.blogspot.com

Cricut Cuteness
cricutcuteness.blogspot.com

Cricut Mania
cricutmania.blogspot.com

Cricut My Way
cricutmyway.blogspot.com

Cricut: The Official Blog
cricutblog.org

DoubleClick Connections
doubleclickconnections.blogspot.com

Eco Green Crafts
ecogreencrafts.com

Funky Cards Created by Madison
funkycards.blogspot.com

Gaby Creates
gabycreates.com

Getting Cricky with K. Andrew
gettingcricky.com

Glora's Crafts
glorascrafts.blogspot.com

Got Scraps?
gotscraps.blogspot.com

HurCraft: Quality Craft Furnishings
hurcraft.com

Jean's Crafty Corner
jeanscraftycorner.blogspot.com

Liz's Paper Loft
lizspaperloft.com

Made by Momo
madebymomo.blogspot.com

Melinda's Paper-Crafting World
& Cooking with Cricut
www.cookingwithcricut.com

Monique Griffith Designs
monkeydoodlecricut.blogspot.
com

My Beautiful, Crazy . . .
Scrappy Life
beautifulcrazyscrappylife.
blogspot.com

My Creative Time
www.creativetimeforme.com

My Cut Search
mycutsearch.com

My Pink Stamper
mypinkstamper.com

Pause Dream Enjoy
pausedreamenjoy.blogspot.com

Peachy Keen Stamps
peachykeenstamps.com

Perfect Paper Crafting
perfectpapercrafting.com

Redheaded Crafter
redheadedcrafter.blogspot.com

Roberts Arts & Crafts
blog.robertscrafts.com

Royal Things
royalthings.blogspot.com

Sandcastle Stamper
sandcastlestamper.blogspot.com

Sassy Scrapper
scrapaholicreations.blogspot.com

Scrap Happens
scraphappenswithrhonda.
blogspot.com

Scrap 'n Tote
scrapntoteblog.com

Scrappin' Navy Wife Nikki
scrappinnavywife.blogspot.com

Scrappin Rabbit Designs
scrappinrabbitdesigns.blogspot.
com

Scrappin' Sista
onescrappinsista.blogspot.com

Scrappy Moms Stamps
scrappymoms-stamps.blogspot.
com

September Ninth
septemberninth.blogspot.com

Serenity Scrappers
serenityscrappers.blogspot.com

She's a Sassy Lady
shesasassylady.blogspot.com

Simply Elegant Paper Crafts
simplyelegantpapercrafts.
blogspot.com

Snappy Scraps
leescraps.blogspot.com

The Cricut Bug
thecricutbug.blogspot.com

The Cropping Canuck
thecroppingcanuck.blogspot.com

Trace-Elementz
trace-elementz.blogspot.com

You Had Me At Craft
youhadmeatcraft.com

SOURCE GUIDE

The following companies manufacture the products featured in this book. If the collection or material is no longer available, you may visit the company's Website for the latest product options. Every attempt has been made to provide proper site information. I apologize to any company not listed or listed incorrectly, and would appreciate hearing from you.

Basic Grey
(801) 544-1116
www.basicgrey.com

Bella Blvd.
(414) 259-1800
www.bellablvd.net

BoBunny Press
(801) 771-4010
www.bobunny.com

Colorbok, Inc.
(800) 366-4660
www.colorbok.com

Core'dinations
www.coredinations.com

Cosmo Cricket
(800) 852-8810
www.cosmocricket.com

Coats & Clark
(800) 648-1479
www.coatsandclark.com

Creative Imaginations
(800) 942-6487
www.cigift.com

Die Cuts With A View
(801) 224-6766
www.diecutswithaview.com

Eco Green Crafts
www.ecogreencrafts.com

Fancy Pants Designs, LLC
(801) 779-3212
www.fancypantsdesigns.com

Fiskars, Inc.
(866) 348-5661
www.fiskars.com

Graphic45
www.g45papers.com

Imaginisce
(888) 908-8111
www.imaginisce.com

K&Company
(888) 244-2083
www.kandcompany.com

Kaiser Craft
www.kaisercraft.net

Little Yellow Bicycle
(860) 286-0244
www.mylyb.com

Martha Stewart Crafts
www.marthastewartcrafts.com

May Arts
www.mayarts.com

My Mind's Eye, Inc.
(800) 665-5116
www.mymindseye.com

My Pink Stamper
www.mypinkstamper.com

Nikki Sivils
www.nikkisivils.com

Paper Studio
(480) 557-5700
www.paperstudio.com

Papertrey Ink
www.papertreyink.com

Petaloo
Petaloo.cameoez.com

Prima Marketing, Inc.
(909) 627-5532
www.primamarketinginc.com

Provo Craft
(800) 937-7686
www.provocraft.com

Reminisce Papers
www.shopreminisce.com

SEI, Inc.
(800) 333-3279
www.shopsei.com

Tattered Angels
(970) 622-9444
www.mytatteredangels.com

Tim Holtz
www.timholtz.com

Tombow
(800) 835-3232
www.tombowusa.com

Tsukineko, Inc.
(800) 769-6633
www.tsukineko.com

We R Memory Keepers, Inc.
(801) 539-5000
www.weronthenet.com

Index

Resources

CREATIVE CUTTING INSPIRATION

For more Cricut projects, instruction, inspiration, and fun, visit some of these creative Cricut users.

Bits of Paper
jamielanedesigns.blogspot.com

BugBites
bugbites411.blogspot.com

Cards by CG: Designs by Cheryl Gaffney
cardsbycg.blogspot.com

Cardz TV
cardztv.blogspot.com

Carson's Creations
carsonscricutcreations.blogspot.com

Cindy's Scraptastic Designs
cindybcreations.blogspot.com

Court's Crafts
courtscrafts.blogspot.com

Craft Junkie Too
www.craftjunkietoo.com

Crafting with Christina
craftingwithcristina.com

Crafting with Katie
craftingwithkatie.com

Crafty Chics
craftychicsblog.blogspot.com

Crazy about Cricut
crazyaboutcricut.blogspot.com

Crazy Card Creator
crazycardcreator.blogspot.com

Create with Expression
expressionbypinke.blogspot.com

Creative Cutter Room
www.creativecutterroom.com

Cricut Couple
cricutcouple.blogspot.com

Cricut Cuteness
cricutcuteness.blogspot.com

Cricut Mania
cricutmania.blogspot.com

Cricut My Way
cricutmyway.blogspot.com

Cricut: The Official Blog
cricutblog.org

DoubleClick Connections
doubleclickconnections.blogspot.com

Eco Green Crafts
ecogreencrafts.com

Funky Cards Created by Madison
funkycards.blogspot.com

Gaby Creates
gabycreates.com

Getting Cricky with K. Andrew
gettingcricky.com

Glora's Crafts
glorascrafts.blogspot.com

Got Scraps?
gotscraps.blogspot.com

HurCraft: Quality Craft Furnishings
hurcraft.com

Jean's Crafty Corner
jeanscraftycorner.blogspot.com

Liz's Paper Loft
lizspaperloft.com

MODES AND FUNCTIONS